PAN STUDY AIDS

CW00953470

COMPUTER STUDIES

Allen Coe

A Pan Original

Pan Books   London and Sydney

First published 1987 by Pan Books Ltd,
Cavaye Place, London SW10 9PG

9 8 7 6 5 4 3 2

ISBN 0 330 29987 5

Text design by Peter Ward
Text illustration by M L Design
Photoset by Parker Typesetting Service, Leicester
Printed and bound in Spain by
Mateu Cromo SA, Madrid

CONTENTS

6 Contents

ACKNOWLEDGEMENTS

I am grateful to the examination boards for permission to reproduce questions from past papers.

The author and publishers wish to thank the following for permission to reprint copyright material: Acorn Computers Ltd for the diagram of the BBC Master on p.44, The British Railways Board for the Prestel pages, on p.124, the Controller of Her Majesty's Stationery Office for an extract from the National Criteria–Computer Studies in the Introduction and Mr J. G. Field for material previously published in *Computer Studies* by J. G. Field and A. Coe.

INTRODUCTION TO GCSE

From 1988, there will be a single system of examining at 16 plus in England, Wales and Northern Ireland. The General Certificate of Secondary Education (GCSE) will replace the General Certificate of Education (GCE) and the Certificate of Secondary Education (CSE). In Scotland candidates will be entering for the O grade and standard grade examinations leading to the award of the Scottish Certificate of Education (SCE).

The Pan Study Aids GCSE series has been specially written by practising teachers and examiners to enable you to prepare successfully for this new examination.

GCSE introduces several important changes in the way in which you are tested. First, the examinations will be structured so that you can show *what* you know rather than what you do *not* know. Of critical importance here is the work you produce during the course of the examination year, which will be given much greater emphasis than before. Second, courses are set and marked by six examining groups instead of the previous twenty GCE/CSE boards. The groups are:

Northern Examining Association (NEA)
Midland Examining Group (MEG)
London and East Anglian Group (LEAG)
Southern Examining Group (SEG)
Welsh Joint Examinations Council (WJEC)
Northern Ireland Schools Examination Council (NISEC)

One of the most useful changes introduced by GCSE is the single award system of grades A–G. This should permit you and future employers more accurately to assess your qualifications.

GCSE	GCE O Level	CSE
A	A	–
B	B	–
C	C	1
D	D	2
E	E	3
F	F	4
G		5

Remember that, whatever examinations you take, the grades you are awarded will be based on how well you have done.

Pan Study Aids are geared for use throughout the duration of your courses. The text layout has been carefully designed to provide all the information and skills you need for GCSE and SCE examinations – please feel free to use the margins for additional notes.

NB Where questions are drawn from former O level examination papers, the following abbreviations are used to identify the boards.

UCLES	AEB
ULSEB	SUJB
O & C	SCE
JMB	SEB

INTRODUCTION TO GCSE COMPUTER STUDIES

The National Criteria for Computer Studies prescribes the common core for each of the examining groups offering GCSE computer studies. This core covers approximately ninety per cent of the total content and it repeatedly emphasizes the practical nature of the subject. In this Pan Study Aid all the major aspects of the Computer Studies GCSE are thoroughly detailed and, whenever appropriate, related to realistic modern applications.

The GCSE syllabuses stress the ability to recognize tasks which are appropriate for computerization and an understanding of the advantages which this will offer and the limitations which it will impose. The accent is not on a detailed grasp of the internal operation of the computer, but on the ability of the candidate to select the most appropriate system specification for a particular application and to use computers sensibly in the solution of practical problems. This Pan Study Aid encourages the development of this ability with clear explanations and relevant questions.

Computer Studies is an interesting and worthwhile course; the use of this Study Aid will greatly facilitate success in the GCSE examination to which it leads.

TEXT ANALYSIS BY EXAMINATION GROUPS

	(1)	(2)	(3)	(4)	(5)
Micro-, Mini- and Mainframe Computers	*	*	*	*	*
The Structure of the Digital Computer	*	*	*	*	*
The Central Processing Unit	*	*	*	*	*
Analogue to Digital Conversion	*	*	*	*	*
A Comparison of Input Devices	*	*	*	*	*

	(1)	(2)	(3)	(4)	(5)
A Comparison of Output Devices	*	*	*	*	*
Immediate Access Storage	*	*	*	*	*
ROMs, PROMs and EPROMs	*	*	*	*	*
Random Access Memory (RAM)	*	*	*	*	*
Backing Storage Devices	*	*	*	*	*
The Binary System	*	*	*	*	*
Character and Integer Representation	*	*	*	*	*
Sign and Magnitude Coding	0	*	0	*	*
Two's Complement	*	*	*	*	*
Logic Gates – NOT, AND, OR.	0	*	*	0	0
Further Logic Gates	0	0	*	0	0
Real Number Representation	0	*	0	*	0
Apparent Arithmetic Errors	*	*	*	*	*
Data Capture	*	*	*	*	*
Encoding	*	*	*	*	*
Verification	*	*	*	*	*
Validation	*	*	*	*	*
Data File Organization	*	*	*	*	*
Data File Management	*	*	*	*	*
File Security	*	*	*	*	*
Machine Code	*	*	*	*	*
Assembly Language	*	*	*	*	*
High Level Languages	*	*	*	*	*
Utility and Applications Packages	*	*	*	*	*
Interpreters and Compilers	*	*	*	*	*
Programming Errors	*	*	*	*	*
Operating Systems	*	*	*	*	*
Types of Computer Operation	*	*	*	*	*
Modems	*	*	*	*	*
Prestel	*	*	*	*	*
Electronic Mail	*	*	*	*	*

	(1)	(2)	(3)	(4)	(5)
Teletext	*	*	*	*	*
Word Processing	*	*	*	*	*
Computer Personnel	*	*	*	*	*
Documentation	*	*	*	*	*
Case Study	*	*	*	*	*
Real Time Applications	*	*	*	*	*
Interactive Applications	*	*	*	*	*
Batch Processing	*	*	*	*	*
The Cashless Society	*	*	*	*	*
Small Business Applications	*	*	*	*	*
Robots	*	*	*	*	*
Weather Forecasting	*	*	*	*	*
Police Computing	*	*	*	*	*
Supermarket Shopping and Stock Control	*	*	*	*	*
Education	*	*	*	*	*
Computers in Society	*	*	*	*	*
Computers and Employment	*	*	*	*	*
The Use of Databases	*	*	*	*	*
The Data Protection Act	*	*	*	*	*
Computer Crime	*	*	*	*	*
Coursework	*	*	*	*	*
Algorithms	*	*	*	*	*
Sort Routines	*	*	*	*	*

*   the topic is included within the relevant examining group syllabus.

⁰   the topic is not included.

(1)   The London and East Anglian Group   (L)

(2)   The Midland Examining Group   (M)

(3)   The Northern Examining Association   (N)

(4)   The Southern Examining Group   (S)

(5)   The Welsh Joint Education Committee   (W)

COMPUTER CONFIGURATION

CONTENTS

MICRO-, MINI- AND MAINFRAME COMPUTERS

An impressive variety of computers is now available to satisfy the requirements of a rapidly expanding range of processing applications. The recognized sizes are:

THE MICROCOMPUTER

The smallest type of computer and now a standard feature in secondary schools, the microcomputer is portable and cheap, costing from as little as £50. Its single processing chip is increasingly powerful and frequently able to cope with the demands of a small business, but it can only be used by one person at a time and will normally require the provision of backing storage. It can generally be used without skilled support.

THE MINICOMPUTER

This is distinguished from the microcomputer by its ability to support a limited number of simultaneous users (10–12). Prices may range from £4000–£5000 up to perhaps ten times these figures. A small staff is needed to operate this computer.

THE MAINFRAME COMPUTER

This is the largest, most powerful type of computer and capable of supporting a much greater number of simultaneous users. It will be operated by a large specialist team, each member having a well-defined responsibility. Such computers cost thousands, even millions of pounds and are rarely found outside the large organizations which have a real demand for their enormous processing power, e.g. the major clearing banks.

As the performance of the smaller computers is extended and greater advantage is taken of linking computers into networks, these distinctions become unclear, particularly as increasingly powerful 'super microcomputers' have now been developed which permit a limited number of simultaneous users. If required to comment on the appropriateness of a particular computer configuration, the student should always consider its **cost** and **capability** in relation to the **specific processing requirement**.

The vast majority of computers are digital computers, that is they represent data and instructions in a **binary code** – for instance, the presence of an electrical pulse to represent 1 and its absence to represent 0. Digital computers are becoming cheaper and their use of numeric codes readily facilitates **general purpose applications. Analogue computers** use variation in a physical quantity to differentiate between the numbers – for example, the larger the electric current the greater the number – but their relative inflexibility, slowness, susceptibility to signal decay and cost are making them increasingly rare.

THE GENERAL STRUCTURE OF THE DIGITAL COMPUTER

All computers share the basic structure shown below (Figure 1.1).

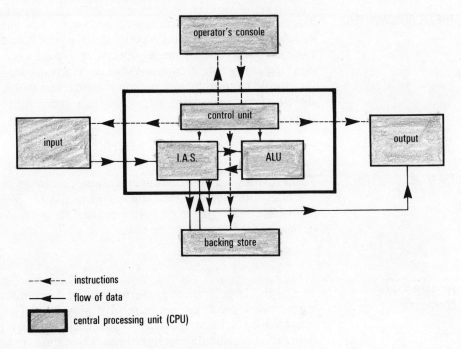

Figure 1.1 The general structure of a digital computer

THE CENTRAL PROCESSING UNIT (CPU)

This consists of three parts:

The control unit which handles the *interpretation* and *execution* of the program instructions. It locates each successive instruction using a **sequence control register** or **program counter** which stores the address of the next instruction to be used; the counter automatically advances when the instruction is obeyed. This unit controls all other parts of the computer and synchronizes their action to ensure the correct execution of the instruction.

The arithmetic and logic unit (ALU) consists of a number of special stores called *registers*. It is able to carry out all arithmetic calculations and logic operations such as comparing the contents of two stores.

The main store is also called the **immediate access store (IAS)**. It stores the *program*, *data* and *current processing results*. The falling price of silicon chips and their greater capacity is being reflected in the steadily increasing size of main storage capability.

The computer units attached to the CPU are called **peripherals**.

Input devices convert information which people can understand into patterns of electrical pulses used by the CPU. **Output devices** reverse this procedure and convert the electrical pulses from the CPU into the required output format.

These physical components of a computer are called hardware. The programs and procedures which it executes are software. 'Firmware' is the term increasingly used to describe software stored on a silicon chip.

ANALOGUE TO DIGITAL CONVERSION

When a digital computer is used to process data originating in an analogue form, the input to the system is provided through an **analogue to digital converter (A–D converter)** (see Figure 1.2).

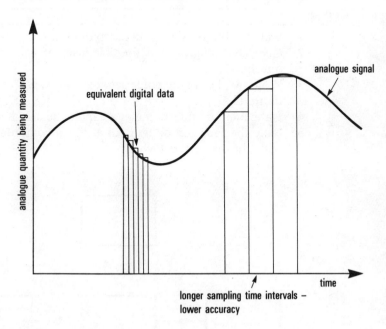

Figure 1.2 Analogue to digital conversion

The analogue signal – for instance the temperature of a furnace – is sampled at frequent intervals and the value fixed at that instant input to the digital computer. In process control applications, the system is extended so that an output from the computer (in digital form) is re-converted to an analogue quantity for actual control, e.g. the opening or closing of a valve.

The operator's console is a feature of mainframe computers and is used by the computer operator to control the computer. It will consist of a keyboard to provide instructions for the computer and a VDU to receive messages from the computer and to monitor its progress.

Backing storage – where the processing requires access to extensive data, the capacity of the IAS alone may be insufficient. Backing storage provides rapid access to **very large amounts** of data.

SUMMARY:	
1	There are three recognized computer sizes: microcomputer, minicomputer and mainframe computer.
2	Almost all computers are digital computers; if analogue input is required, the signal is first passed through an analogue to digital converter.
3	The heart of the computer is the central processing unit (CPU), which consists of three parts; the control unit, the arithmetic and logic unit and the main store.

CHAPTER 1 QUESTIONS

1 State the three recognized computer sizes.
2 Give an example of a possible user of each type of computer in question 1.
3 Why are the distinctions between the types of computer becoming blurred?
4 Is the mercury thermometer an analogue or a digital device?
5 State the four components of a digital computer. Use them to complete the diagram below.

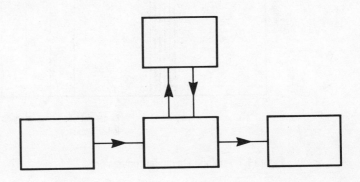

6   What do the letters CPU represent?

7   Three parts of the CPU of a computer are given below. Explain the function of each part.
    (a)   control unit
    (b)   logical processing unit
    (c)   main store   (N)

8   Distinguish between computer hardware and computer software.

9   Why is backing storage necessary in most computer systems?

10 Use this text to find an example of a computer process which requires analogue to digital conversion.

INPUT AND OUTPUT METHODS

CONTENTS

Applications are the key to success. GCSE examination questions will require you to select the most appropriate input and/or output method (possibly from a list), and to justify that selection by detailing its superiority in comparison with other possible devices or techniques for the specified application.

INPUT

Rapid technological advances and sophisticated software have focused attention on direct communication with the computer, e.g. the touch-sensitive screen. Nevertheless, many computer applications require the transfer of information from a **source document**, e.g. a driving licence application, to a suitable medium for computer input, e.g. magnetic tape. A variety of **devices**, e.g. the punched card reader, read the data from these **media** and translate it into a series of electrical pulses used by the CPU.

PUNCHED CARDS AND PAPER TAPE

Punched cards and paper tape were the first commercial storage mediums, but are VERY rarely used in modern systems.

The standard punched card is divided into 80 columns and 12 rows. Each column represents a **single character** in binary code so that hole = 1 and no hole = 0. Figure 2.1 shows the structure of the card with the digit and alphabet punches. The card is read vertically, e.g. A = 100100000000.

Figure 2.1 The punched card

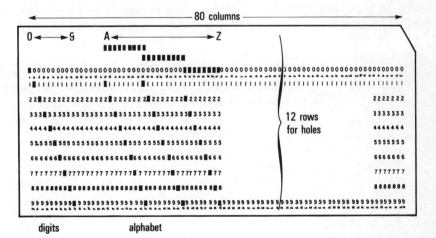

Kimball tags are small punched cards used by some retail stores to record sales details. The tags contain a full description of the article (size, colour, style etc.) and its manufacturer. They are removed **at the time of sale** and either batched together for later processing at the computer centre (**batch processing**) or read by a special card reader at the point of sale, which transfers the details to magnetic tape or disc. The individual details will simplify re-ordering and the complete record will be used for periodical sales and stock analysis.

Figure 2.2 The Kimball tag

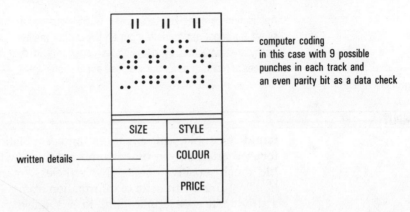

computer coding in this case with 9 possible punches in each track and an even parity bit as a data check

written details

Paper tape employs the same binary code principle. The width of the tape is divided into eight possible punching positions or tracks. Seven positions are used to encode the number or character (ASCII code) and the eighth is reserved for the *parity bit*. The purpose of the parity track is to ensure either an even number of holes – *even parity* –or an odd number of holes – *odd parity* – in every frame.

Figure 2.3 Punched paper tape

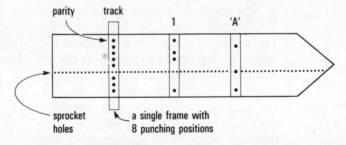

This is a simple validation procedure (see p.77) or data check. If a frame with incorrect parity is reached during processing an error will be registered. Figure 2.3 shows a section of 8-track (7-data bit) paper tape; the characters are represented using even parity.

Punched card and paper tape readers translate the pattern of holes into an equivalent series of electronic pulses by allowing a beam of light to shine through each hole of a frame. It is then registered by a photo-electronic cell corresponding to that position.

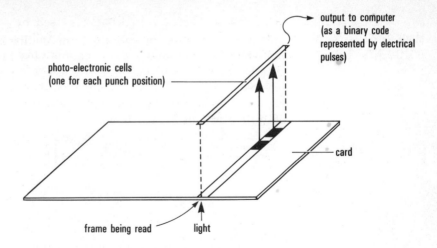

output to computer
(as a binary code
represented by electrical
pulses)

photo-electronic cells
(one for each punch position)

card

Figure 2.4 Reading a
punched card

frame being read   light

COMPARISON OF PUNCHED CARD AND PAPER TAPE

1 **Cost** Paper tape is cheaper, despite the need to produce two tapes (for verification), whereas only one card is required.
2 **Storage** Paper tape stores data more efficiently and the tapes themselves are more easily stored than the bulky cards.
3 **Usage** Punched cards are more flexible, any error requiring the replacement of a single card. A similar error on paper tape would require the whole tape to be re-punched.
4 **Speed** The reading speed ranges are approximately the same, with the fastest readers both operating around 2,000 cps (characters per second).

THE KEYBOARD

The keyboard looks like an electronic typewriter; despite attempts to introduce improved keyboard designs, it normally incorporates the standard QWERTY keyboard (after the first letters of the top row of keys) and additional special function keys. It can be used to:

(*a*)   supply **data** and **instructions** directly to the computer
(*b*)   type data to magnetic disc or tape (**key-to-disc** and **key-to-tape**). In this case the medium is used later to provide the CPU with data at electronic speeds. **The keyboard is the most frequently used input method.**

The transfer of information from source documents is **expensive**, **time consuming** and **subject to human error**. **Document readers** omit this stage by reading the source document and inputting data directly to the CPU.

MARK SENSE DOCUMENTS

This process requires pre-printed forms so that marks can be read in predetermined positions; it is commonly used to mark multi-choice examinations or to encode information where a simple option may be selected, e.g. football pools, hospital meal orders. Figure 2.5 shows a section of an examination answer sheet; candidates must choose one of the five options in each question.

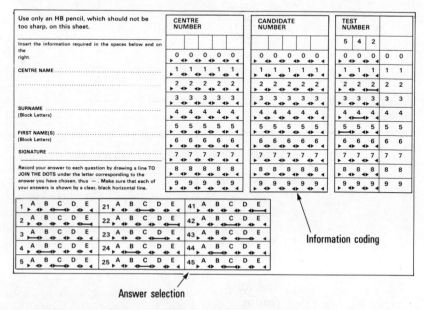

Figure 2.5 Examination multichoice answer sheet

The mark sense reader identifies shading in predetermined positions by the amount of light which is reflected (light reflected = no mark). When using this method it is vital that the marks are sufficiently dark. The process is called optical mark recognition.

OPTICAL CHARACTER RECOGNITION

Optical character readers incorporate a video camera which scans the page and identifies each character by the pattern of reflected light. If a **standardized font** (special printing style) is used, this process combines rapid reading speeds with high levels of accuracy.

OCR is now applied to some word processing systems; an ordinary typewriter is used and the data is read directly to the computer by an optical character reader made to decode that particular print style. The most advanced systems now employ vast silicon chip storage to decipher handwriting by comparing it with numerous 'standard' patterns. This technique is not yet sufficiently accurate for widespread commercial application.

OCR and mark sensing are frequently combined in the production of common **household bills** which requires the customers' co-operation in using a **turnaround document**.

AN OUTPUT DOCUMENT WHICH LATER IS USED AS AN INPUT DOCUMENT WHEN DATA IS ADDED TO IT.

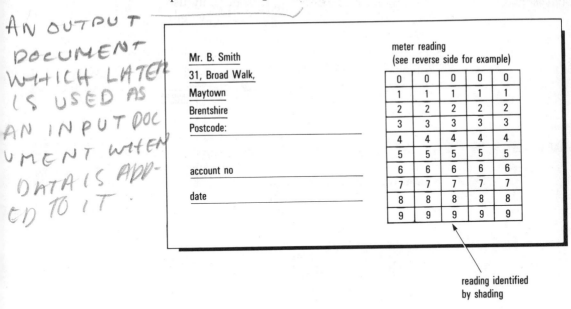

Figure 2.6 Turnaround document

The form, pre-printed by computer, has space to record the meter reading (in a similar way to the multi-choice test answers). After being returned, the name and account details are input directly to the computer by an OCR reader and the corresponding meter reading is input by mark sensing. In similar systems OCR alone is used to recognize both typed and handwritten characters.

Figure 2.7 Cheque characters

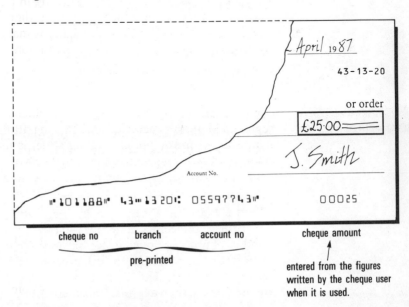

MAGNETIC INK CHARACTERS

Magnetic ink characters are used extensively by the Clearing Banks. The characters are printed on to cheques in an ink which can be magnetized using a stylized font which allows the information to be read by both man and machine. The reading device is a magnetic ink character reader (MICR); it distinguishes the characters by the area of magnetic ink used. The process, *magnetic ink character recognition*, is very fast and extremely accurate.

BAR CODES

A bar code is a group of lines of various thicknesses and spacing (see Figure 2.8) which represents a binary code. The code is read using a **light wand** or a **laser scanner**.

Figure 2.8 A bar code

Such codes have been rapidly adopted for retail pricing. They contain a full description of the item and its manufacturer (for stock control). At the time of purchase the price of the item is automatically registered from the computer's memory at the point-of-sale terminal. Using this system, many stores are now able to provide itemized receipts.

Bar codes are also used extensively in large libraries. By reading the bar code on the borrower's membership card and the book(s), an instant detailed record of the loan is made.

BADGE READERS

A badge is the general name for a piece of plastic, similar to a credit card, which contains data. The data is usually magnetic, but it could be optical or simply punched holes. The card normally enables the user to identify himself to the system in order to gain access to either property or services, e.g. a bank cash card.

Some countries are introducing this system in public telephones, e.g. British Telecom Phonecard. A card is purchased to provide a number of units of time (20, 40, 100 and 200 on the phonecard) which the terminal displays. As the call proceeds units are cancelled, i.e. the card is 'written to'. The card can be used repeatedly until all the units are used and it then expires.

The significant use of computers **interactively** has led to the development of other input devices specifically designed for this mode of operation:

THE MOUSE

The mouse is a small, rounded cuboid. A ball is set into its base and any movement of the mouse on a **flat surface** is registered by a **corresponding movement of the screen cursor**. The mouse is normally used in conjunction with **screen icons** (small pictorial symbols). The user selects the icon which corresponds to the action he requires by moving the cursor into the icon area and pressing the execute button.

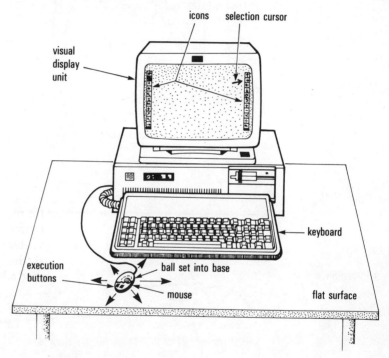

Figure 2.9 Mouse, icons and computer

Sophisticated software packages are now enabling the mouse to be used to promote artistic design and creation. The design can be honed to completion using a variety of shading techniques (selected as icons) and rapidly viewed in a wide range of colours. On completion, it may be printed out in colour if required, using a screen dump routine and/or stored on magnetic (floppy) disc.

Advanced software development with split screen options permit the use of, say, word processing and spreadsheet packages simultaneously; the mouse can be used to select the result of a spreadsheet calculation and incorporate it in the word processing material. **Joysticks** (or **games paddles**) are used in a similar way to provide the rapid multi-directional movement often demanded by computer games.

THE TOUCH SENSITIVE SCREEN

This also displays icons – the screen is simply touched to execute the option. One application of this technique is the automatic dialling of telephone numbers in busy offices by touching the screen area displaying the required name or destination.

Figure 2.9a Touch sensitive screen display

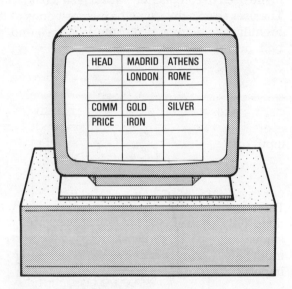

Figure 2.10 A digitizer

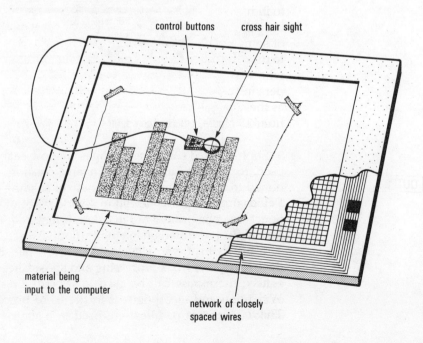

Touch sensitive technology is also employed in the **graphics tablet** (or pad). A network of extremely close horizontal and vertical wires beneath a partially conductive writing surface identifies the movement of a stylus over the surface using (x,y) co-ordinates. These are input directly to the computer and the corresponding line displayed on the VDU. This technique could be used for freehand work or to 'copy' a diagram into the computer. It is also the basis for **dynamic character recognition**, in which a high-speed microprocessor is used to identify handwritten characters as they are entered.

Alternatively, plans or design work could be input to the computer, using a **digitizer** which transmits the current (x,y) co-ordinates (identified by a crossed-hair sight) to the computer.

THE LIGHT PEN

A basic design can be modified using a light pen. By detecting the electron beam which constantly refreshes the VDU display, the operator is able to 'draw' directly on the screen, i.e. data is directly input to the computer (see Figure 2.17).

VOICE INPUT

This is now a realistic possibility for some **limited vocabulary** applications, but the uniqueness of individual voice-prints still poses a problem yet to be solved on a commercial scale. Nevertheless, this form of input is so convenient that it is certain to be of great future importance.

Many of the input techniques have been developed in direct response to industrial or commercial applications – for instance, the light pen – but others have been developed from a recognition of the limitations of some users. The mouse, for example, largely overcomes the need to use keyboard skills and may therefore promote confidence in those who wish to use computers but lack these skills. Some handicapped persons cannot use a keyboard and alternative input methods, such as the concept keyboard – which replaces the keyboard with a limited number of responses – are particularly valuable.

OUTPUT

Rapid computer and peripheral development now enables the user to select the most appropriate form of output. Factors which may be taken into consideration include:

1 The **purpose** of the output – computers are used increasingly in control applications where readable output is not required.
2 Is **hard copy** required?
3 Will it be necessary to **interrogate computer held files**?
4 The **cost** and **speed** of the device.

5   The **flexibility** of the device – will it, for example, offer a good range of characters and graphics?

PRINTERS

Printers provide a **hardcopy** (printout) of the program output. They use either **continuous paper** – moved through the printer by friction or sprocket drives – or cut paper fed to the printer using a special hopper. Continuous paper with micro-perforations (giving a clean edge) combines the faster output of continuous paper with the need to produce letter quality documents.

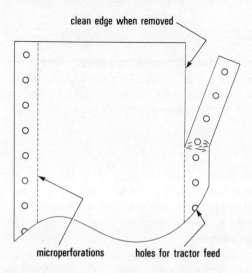

clean edge when removed

microperforations   holes for tractor feed

Figure 2.11 Continuous stationery (clean edge)

SINGLE CHARACTER PRINTERS

These print one character in each operation and move along the line like a typewriter. They are the cheapest and slowest machines.

TELETYPE

This is the most basic, operating at around 10 cps and producing low quality print on cheap continuous paper. It is an impact printer, i.e. there is physical contact between the printing head and the paper. This inevitably causes wear and a level of noise unacceptable in modern offices. They are now rarely found.

DAISYWHEEL PRINTER

The cylindrical or golfball printing head is replaced by a circular wheel whose spokes are embossed with the characters. Daisywheels produce a much higher quality of print and are commonly found in **word processing systems**. They operate at 25–40 cps.

Figure 2.12 A daisywheel

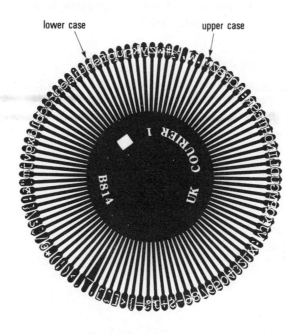

lower case   upper case

DOT MATRIX PRINTER

The dot matrix printer is not based on embossed character; instead the printing head consists of a number of 'pins' (usually 9) in a vertical column which, when struck selectively, form the outline of a single character. The printing speed varies with the **output quality**; **low quality drafting** up to 180 cps and normal correspondence 90–100 cps (three times as fast as the daisywheel). **NLQ (near letter quality) requires 'double' printing** to fill the gap between the original dots; this provides excellent print quality, but cuts the speed to approximately **30 cps**.

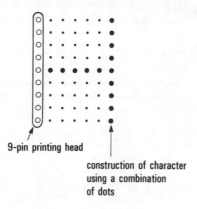

9-pin printing head

construction of character
using a combination
of dots

Figure 2.13 Dot matrix printing

These printers are **bi-directionl**, have a limited **graphics capability** and some can print in up to 8 'colours'. Their low cost and versatility make them ideal for many applications which require limited hard copy, such as small businesses and schools.

THE LINE PRINTER

A line printer produces a complete line in a single operation, using either a **chain** or **barrel** embossed with the characters. A single line of print is created by a single revolution of the barrel or circuit of the chain.

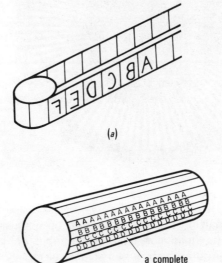

(a)

(b)   a complete
            row for each letter

Figure 2.14 Chain and barrel

The chain printer has a hammer in each printing position which strikes the fast revolving chain at the correct instant. The barrel printer also has a separate hammer for each character position, but the barrel has a complete row of each character and it is printed **throughout** the line (see Figure 2.15). In practice the printer will not always begin with 'A', but with the letter nearest the print head at that time.

					A													
				B	A													
		E		B	A		E											
	H	E		B	A		E						I			E		
	H	E		B	A		E	L					I			E		
	H	E		B	A		E	L					I	N		E		
	H	E		B	A		E	L			P		I	N		E		
	H	E		B	A	R	R	E	L			P	R	I	N		E	R
T	H	E		B	A	R	R	E	L			P	R	I	N	T	E	R

Figure 2.15 How a barrel printer constructs a phrase

Line printers are very noisy and much more expensive than character-based printers. They are employed where a higher volume of printing is necessary and often use special pre-printed stationery, e.g. billing applications such as Local Authority rate demand notices.

NON-IMPACT PRINTERS

The main advantage of non-impact printers is their virtually silent operation; the main disadvantage is their cost.

Thermal printers use expensive aluminiumized or chemically impregnated papers. The top surface is selectively 'burned' away (using the dot matrix principle) to reveal a character on the backing paper. Some recent hand-held computer terminals incorporate restricted width thermal printers.

Ink jet printers spray ink through a series of very fine nozzles to form the character. The print quality is very high and an extensive colour range is available.

Laser printers use a computer controlled laser beam to etch characters on to a light-sensitive drum. The character image can then be coated with ink and printed. Such printers can operate at 200 pages per minute, but are relatively expensive.

The complete set of characters and symbols which a computer can represent is called its **character set**.

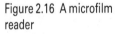

Figure 2.16 A microfilm reader

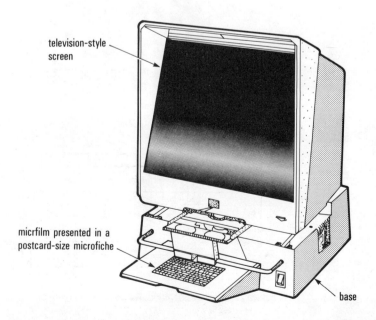

television-style screen

micrfilm presented in a postcard-size microfiche

base

COMPUTER OUTPUT ON MICROFILM (COM)

An increasingly used 'coded' form of output is microfilm. Microfilm can now be made **directly** from magnetic tape (it was previously printed and photographed) and is able to store vast quantities of information in a very small area. The film is usually cut into postcard-size sections (**microfiche**) which contain 200–300 pages. It is already popular in banking, libraries and vehicle manufacture, despite the need for special reading equipment (see Figure 2.16).

THE VISUAL DISPLAY UNIT (VDU)

The VDU is an essential feature of modern computer systems. It looks like a television and offers a number of advantages:

1 It is **fast**-operating at around 1000 cps, making it ideal for file interrogation.
2 It offers a **very flexible** output which includes both colour and graphics capability.
3 It is **clean** and **quiet** for office use.

It cannot offer hard copy but computer arrangements now provide both VDUs and printers so that expensive paper is only used for the final hard copy.

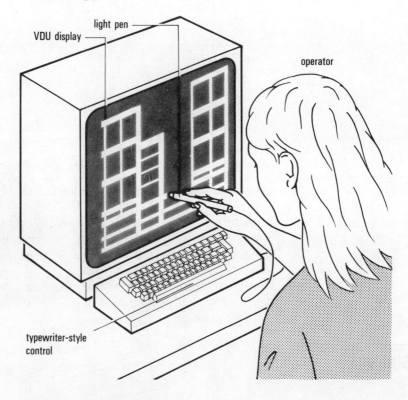

Figure 2.17 Computer aided design

COMPUTER AIDED DESIGN (CAD)

The use of the VDU has become important in the field of computer aided design. Using a **light pen** it is possible to change any design, request a cross-section or to 'see' the object from a variety of views. For high definition the VDU may be replaced by a **graphics display unit (GDU)**. Similar in appearance, it has a much **higher resolution** – the number of individual pixels (picture cells) which form the screen.

Some systems use the finished design directly in the manufacturing stage (it is then the input), but alternatively, a hard copy could be obtained using a graph plotter, of which there are two types:

1 **Flat bed (X–Y) plotter**
2 **Drum plotter**

Both of these peripherals provide full-size drawings, but in the first the paper is kept still whilst the pen moves in all directions, while in the latter the paper moves backwards and forwards and the pen from side to side.

ACOUSTIC OUTPUT

Computers can **simulate** the voice by either using pre-recorded words – and making them into sentences – or phonemes (very small sound units) to generate speech. This form of output is finding a number of applications, particularly as a warning device and as an educational tool. It is incorporated in some car specifications and by Texas Instruments in their Speak 'n' Spell machine designed to teach young children spelling. It could be extremely useful in reading to blind people. Speech synthesis ROMs are now available for some microcomputers, including the BBC.

Similarly, sophisticated music synthesizers provide excellent simulation of both individual instruments and their combination.

OUTPUT BUFFERS

All printers are 'connected' to the computer via an output buffer. This is because the CPU operates at a much higher speed than the printer; after loading the buffer, it is then able to continue processing while the buffer drives the output device. If the output device is particularly slow, e.g. a graph plotter (sometimes called a digital plotter), it is possible to store the output from the computer on magnetic disc or tape and have it printed by a device not connected to the computer (**off-line printing**).

SUMMARY:

1 Punched cards and paper tape are **rarely** found in today's computing systems.

2 The keyboard is the **most frequently** used input method.

3   Modern computing systems are increasingly using input techniques which read source documents and codes directly. These include:

Input technique	Application
Optical character recognition	word processing and billing applications
Mark sense recognition	multichoice exams and football pool selection
MICR	bank cheques
Bar codes	retail pricing
Badge readers	cash point cards, phone cards

4   The increasing use of computers interactively has fostered the development of input devices specifically designed for this mode of operation. These include:

Device	Application
The mouse	with an icon-based menu in preference to the keyboard
Graphics tablet	freehand work or copying a design from paper
Digitizer	the accurate transfer of a design original to the computer
Light pen	computer aided design

5   The VDU is used extensively for both input (with a keyboard) and output when a hard copy is not required.

6   Printers vary greatly in cost and specification. The three major types are:

Daisywheel – slow, high quality, used for correspondence.

Dot Matrix – can be faster depending on quality selection, general purpose for limited output applications.

Line Printer – much faster and more expensive, mediocre print quality, large scale (billing) applications.

7   Acoustic output (speech synthesis) is used both as a warning mechanism and in special computing applications.

8   Computer Output on Microfilm (COM) is increasingly popular where vast amounts of data must be stored.

9   Buffers are used during the output process because of the difference in speed between the CPU and the output device.

CHAPTER 2 QUESTIONS

1 Name six distinct devices used for computer input. (N)
2 Which computing device might be used in the design of a car?
3 What is a parity bit? Why is it used? How is the correct parity checked **during processing**?
4 What is the most frequently used method of input?
5 How do the processes of optical mark recognition and optical character recognition differ? State an application for each process.
6 Why might an artist have a preference for a mouse as an input device?
7 Suggest an application which could use a digitizer for input to the computer and a graph plotter for output.
8 State three types of printer and an application for each type.
9 Give two advantages and two disadvantages of the use of the visual display unit as an output device.
10 Why are output buffers used?
11 Use the following list to complete the sentences:

laser scanner
microfiche
modem
mouse
OCR reader
OMR reader

(a) Barcode labels can be read by a
(b) Graphics design is easier using a
(c) Turnaround documents, e.g. gas bill, can be read by a

(d) Multiple choice exam answer sheets can be read by a

(e) Computers can be linked by telephone, using a

(f) Details of books in a library can be stored on
(L)

12 Look carefully at these characters.

"096605"' 30''9l63l: 0306692"' .'00000001999.'

(a) Where would characters like these be printed?
(b) How are these characters read?
(c) What name is given to the method of reading them?
(W)

STORAGE

CONTENTS

Computers use two types of storage
(i)   **Immediate Access Storage**
(ii)   **Backing Storage**

IMMEDIATE ACCESS STORAGE (IAS)

The immediate access store – or **main store** – is a part of the CPU (see Figure 1.1) and it must provide very fast (one millionth of a second) access to any bit of data.

Computers now use **semi-conductor storage chips**. Storage chips were introduced in the mid-1970s and rapidly replaced magnetic core storage which is now found in few surviving systems.

The core memory consists of an array of small ferrite rings which can be magnetized in a clockwise (1) or anticlockwise (0) direction. The rings had to be individually threaded with two 'writing' wires, a separate 'read' wire and sometimes a fourth 'inhibit' wire to restore the correct magnetization after reading.

MEMORY CHIPS

These have a number of advantages:
1   memory chips are much **cheaper** to manufacture and faster in operation (64K RAM chips now cost under 50 pence each);
2   they are **smaller**; the same amount of data can be stored in a much smaller space;
3   they use much **smaller electric current**;
4   the chips are more versatile – extra storage can be added on to various computer designs when required.

Most computers contain two types of storage chip:
1   Read Only Memory (ROM);
2   Random Access Memory (Ram).
It is a common mistake to think of ROM and RAM as opposites. This is not the case; read-only chips are usually random access.

ROM (read only memory) is **non-volatile** storage – the contents will be retained even if the computer is switched off – and it is used to store the **unchanging** routines which the computer requires. e.g. operating instructions and the decoder for its programming language. Development of the principle has led to a number of ROM chips in common use:

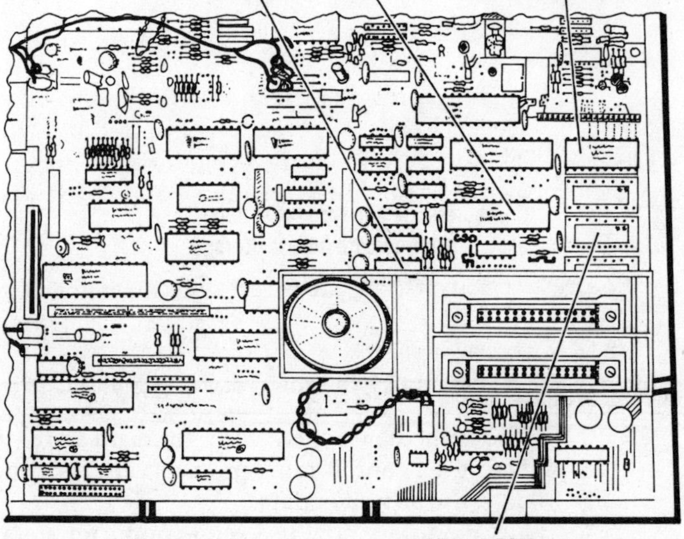

Figure 3.1 The chips of the BBC Master Computer

1 **ROM**: the basic chip, programmed during its manufacture with its stored bits permanently fixed.
2 **PROM** (programmable ROM): also permanent storage, but fixed during the stage of computer assembly.
3 **EPROM** (erasable programmable ROM): this chip offers greater flexibility, but it must be removed from its normal location for reprogramming.
4 **EAROM** (electrically alterable ROM): a further development which uses an increased electric current to reprogramme the chip in its normal position.

RAM (**random access memory**) chips combine with ROM chips to give the overall computer specification. RAM chips can be both **'written to'** and **'read from'** by the user and they are there for his work. The ability to add on further RAM chips is called the expandability of the system. Each memory operates as a transistorized switch and relies on either:
1 **a flip-flop arrangement** which offers stable storage of 0 or 1 until this is changed by the operator; *or*
2 **dynamic storage** where the memory – like the image on a television screen – must be constantly refreshed, i.e. each stored bit is regularly renewed. It is possible that the flicker caused by the periodic refreshment of the VDU screen is related to the headaches and eye-strain from which users of VDUs over consistently long periods have complained. Adequate lighting and a correct working position are essential for such users.

In both cases the memory is **volatile** – the contents are lost if the power supply is interrupted for even the briefest of moments.

The term **random access** means that any individual memory location can be accessed directly without the need to read data in other locations first. When this is necessary – i.e. the time for reading specified data depends on its position – the access is **serial**. The difference between these methods of storage is best compared with the storage of music on a cassette or gramophone record. On a record any song, anywhere on the surface, can be immediately selected, but on a cassette tape the access is strictly sequential so that, to reach a particular song, the earlier ones must first be passed. This can be very important when the required data is stored at the end of a serial access medium.

The size of the main store is limited. It is used to hold only the programs and data **actually being processed** by the CPU. Some extremely sophisticated operating systems make the immediate access store seem larger that it actually is by storing the data required by the program being executed not in the IAS, but on magnetic disc. The data is transferred to the main store as required and the displaced data returned to the magnetic disc. This technique, familiar in mainframe applications, is now being developed for the microcomputer and it is called **virtual storage management**.

BACKING STORAGE

Backing storage supplements the IAS by:

1 **storing vast quantities of data** – with very swift access when it is required.

2 **providing permanent (non-volatile) storage** – the volatile nature of RAM chip storage has ensured the continuing need for efficient backing storage mediums.

Virtually all backing storage uses **magnetic mediums** sharing the same basic principle. A thin film of magnetic oxide covers the core of the medium and this can be magnetized in two directions – north-south or south-north – creating a binary code for 0 and 1.

MAGNETIC TAPE

Magnetic tape systems are still found on **mainframe and minicomputers**. They consist of a reel-to-reel design similar to that used for recording popular music, but with a wider (½″) tape.

The tape is divided into nine tracks of which eight are used to record data bits and the ninth acts as a **parity check** (see p.59). The tape is read vertically and magnetic spots magnetized N–S or S–N create the required binary pattern.

The storage capacity of the tape varies with **packing density** i.e. how

Figure 3.2 Magnetic tape drive

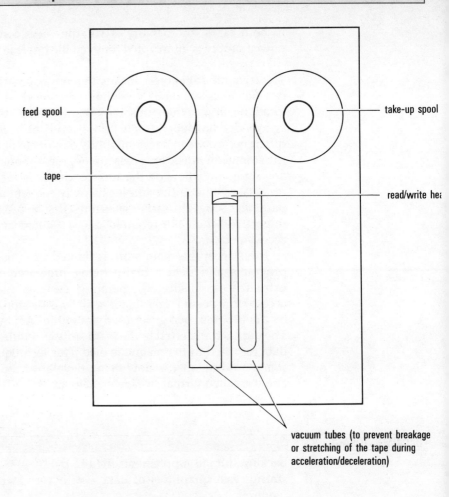

feed spool — take-up spool

tape — read/write hea

vacuum tubes (to prevent breakage
or stretching of the tape during
acceleration/deceleration)

Figure 3.3 Magnetic tape section

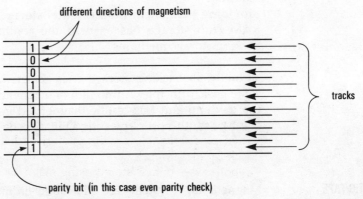

different directions of magnetism

tracks

parity bit (in this case even parity check)

closely the characters are placed together; but for a standard 750-metre tape it would be reasonable to expect to store at least 20 megabytes (a megabyte – abbreviated to Mbyte – is a million bytes, and one byte is the number of bits required to represent a single character) and with extreme packing density it could hold in excess of 100 Mbytes. **The transfer rate** – how quickly the data is sent to the

CPU – is similarly controlled by the speed at which the tape is designed to move over the read-write heads; typically, it is between 100,000 and 200,000 cps.

Problems associated with the use of magnetic tape include the tendency of the read-write heads to be affected by dust and the risk of the tape itself breaking, but the main disadvantage **is where** the data is stored – **access is strictly serial**. This fact, along with the falling prices and customer orientation of disc systems, has encouraged the replacement of magnetic tape systems with disc based systems. Magnetic tape is best used in repetitive, sequential processing where the data can be read in the order it was written, e.g. payroll systems. In addition, the still **relatively low cost** of magnetic tape makes it the ideal medium for **security copies**; in some applications it is used as a back-up for a disc based system.

TAPE CASSETTES

One specialist area of magnetic tape storage is in the use of ordinary music cassettes with home microcomputers. This use of cassettes offers cheap but effective storage; many support programs and games are already marketed to the home user in this form. Although the data is held in magnetic forms on the cassette, it is transmitted to the computer in audio form with a bleep in a specific time interval to indicate a 1 and no bleep to indicate a 0.

A recent tape-based development for the microcomputer is the **microdrive** in which a continuous loop of tape can store up to 100K. Though faster than a cassette, access is still much slower than from floppy disc units and their falling price may well inhibit further microdrive development.

MAGNETIC DISCS

There are two types of storage discs:
1 **Hard discs** – metal core covered by a thin film of magnetic oxide. Such discs are now integrated into the vast majority of modern mainframed and minicomputer systems.
2 **Floppy discs** – plastic core covered by a thin film of magnetic oxide. The most popular storage medium for microcomputer systems, but often also available on both mini- and mainframe computers for back-up file storage.
   In both cases data is stored using magnetic spots (like magnetic tape) on circular tracks written concentrically on the surface of the disc, which is also divided into sectors. The rapid speed of rotation and accessibility of the whole surface effectively provides direct access to any bit of information.

HARD DISCS

These are usually grouped together on a central spindle to form a **disc** pack consisting of six discs. Both sides of the disc are coated with magnetic oxide, but the two exposed outer surfaces are not used, so that a total of 10 surfaces remain available for storage. These surfaces each have a separate read–write head capable of covering the entire surface. During the reading process, there is no physical contact between the read–write head and the surface of the disc and therefore no wearing of the disc surface.

These disc packs are often removable from the disc transport and can be stored in their own plastic cover. Although this may seem an advantage over fixed-disc systems, modern computer installations often require considerable data to be on-line, and the **flexibility** of the **exchangeable disc pack** must be weighed against the **high data densities possible only with fixed-disc systems**.

Figure 3.4 Disc pack

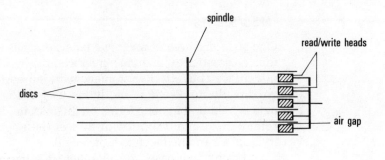

To further reduce access time, some disc systems are equipped with a separate read–write head for each track, thus eliminating the need for 'travel' (search time). In some cases, for additional protection, the read–write heads are sealed in the pack.

The disc pack has impressive storage capacity: 50 to 500 Mbytes. This is combined with rapid access time (as low as 10 milliseconds) to any bit of data and a transfer rate which also exceeds that of magnetic tape. Disc backing storage is used extensively in banking, where rapid access to individual account information is required, and in other applications where **speed is a dominant factor**, e.g. travel enquiries, police national computer enquiries.

FLOPPY DISCS

These are **smaller** and **cheaper** than hard discs. They are flexible and permanently encased in a protective sleeve into which a slot is cut to permit the read–write process. In this case there is contact with the disc during the read–write process and therefore some wear, but in practice the handling of the disc tends to determine its useful life.

Floppy discs can be single- or double-sided and single or double density – how closely the magnetic spots are placed on the tracks – allowing them to hold betweem 100K and 1000K (K is generally accepted as 1000 bytes, but its correct value is $2^{10}=1024$ bytes) with an access time around 200 milliseconds. The 'standard' floppy disc has a

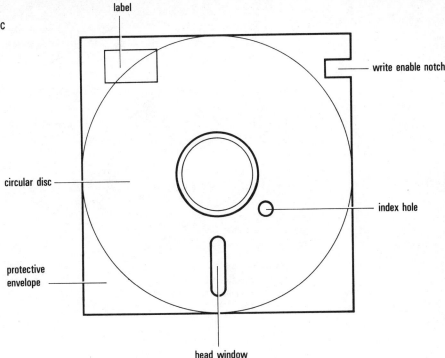

Figure 3.5 Floppy disc

label

write enable notch

circular disc

index hole

protective
envelope

head window

diameter of 5.25 inches but the more recent, relatively high capacity (500K per side) 3.5 inch mini-floppy is increasingly preferred.

Before being used the disc is **formatted** – the process of creating the tracks and sectors on its surface – normally to either 40 or 80 tracks on each side of the disc to be used. Floppy discs are used widely in education and small business applications (see 'Devonbride', chapter 9), but the recently developed **hard disc cartridges** may ultimately provide greater storage capacity at a cheaper price.

WINCHESTER DISC DRIVES

Named after the original IBM reference 3030, they are approximately the same size as a floppy disc drive but, by using a metal disc core, the capacity is greatly increased (currently up to 20 Mbytes) and access time is reduced.

The units are **permanently sealed** to keep the unit dust-free and the discs are mounted on a central spindle. They are ideal for the serious microcomputer user wishing to store large or increasing amounts of data, such as an expanding business – perhaps already using microcomputers – where a large number of floppy discs with scattered business details would be inefficient. In addition they can be found in mini- and mainframe systems for all-purpose data storage.

Figure 3.6 The Winchester
disc drive

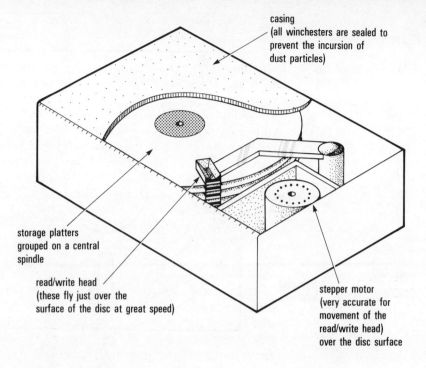

casing
(all winchesters are sealed to
prevent the incursion of
dust particles)

storage platters
grouped on a central
spindle

read/write head
(these fly just over the
surface of the disc at great speed)

stepper motor
(very accurate for
movement of the
read/write head)
over the disc surface

MAGNETIC DRUMS

A form of backing storage used on mainframe computers but rarely
incorporated into modern computer systems. They operate in a very
similar way to magnetic discs. The outer surface of the cylinder is
coated with magnetic oxide and divided into circular tracks.

Figure 3.7 Magnetic drum

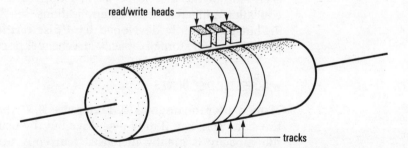

read/write heads

tracks

The drums are permanently positioned and read by a separate read–
write head for every track which, combined with the high speed of
rotation, gives swift access to any bit of data – making them ideal for
database interrogation applications. The storage capacity of the
drums varies with length, diameter and the packing of the tracks, but
is generally between 1 and 10 Mbytes.

RECENT DEVELOPMENTS

BUBBLE MEMORY CHIPS The bubbles (magnetic cylinders) are formed in a crystalline material such as garnet, and hold a magnetic charge opposite to that of the surrounding material. The presence of a bubble in any store indicates a 1 and its absence indicates a 0. The bubbles are moved around the chip so quickly that the storage is effectively **random access**. The bubble memory is **non-volatile, high capacity** (up to 1 million bits in a standard chip) and, being **solid state**, unaffected by its environment (e.g. temperature, humidity). Development difficulties remain, but the bubble storage chip might ultimately replace some current storage methods.

VIDEODISCS (OR OPTICAL DISCS) These use microscopic pits beneath the surface of the disc to store a digitally encoded signal, which can be **read by a laser beam**. They offer **enormous storage capacity** – far greater than a smaller magnetic disc – but at present they do **not have the 'write' facility** which would ensure their extensive use in computer systems. Nevertheless interactive video techniques, which utilize a microcomputer together with an optical disc player, are already being developed for **industrial training applications**.

The incorporation of the microcomputer enables the trainer to select sections, or even individual 'still' frames, **in any sequence**; reading by laser ensures absolute accuracy and, with random access to the disc, data transfer is virtually instantaneous. By using an **authoring language** such as MICROTEXT the display can be interrupted with questions to create a complete training structure. Incorrect responses could be supported by branching techniques to review earlier sections or to reinforce particular points.

The videodisc was the medium selected for the marketing of the Domesday Project to schools and colleges. It allows a vast amount of information to be interrogated by the user.

Figure 3.8 Microcomputer and videodisc system

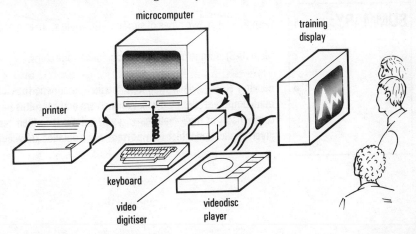

The incorporation of a **digitizer** into the system would enable hard copy of the VDU display to be obtained. Furthermore, the dual soundtrack could be dubbed differently so that the same pictures could be seen with different commentary – a particularly useful feature for the teaching of languages.

Figure 3.9 Sample output from a digitizer

The potential of this type of system is, as yet, little developed. A major problem is the high cost of mastering a disc, which inevitably is reflected in the retail price.

SUMMARY:

1 Computers use two types of storage – the main store and backing storage.

2 Main (IAS) storage uses semi-conductor storage chips.

3 Backing storage uses magnetic media – magnetic tape and disc for mainframe and minicomputers; floppy discs, Winchesters and cassettes for microcomputers. A general comparison of their features is given below; **it is their relative appropriateness for a given application which is important**, not a detailed knowledge of specifications.

Medium	Comparison
Magnetic tape	Large capacity Slow serial access Slower transfer rate than magnetic disc Still cheaper than magnetic disc
Magnetic disc pack	Very large capacity Rapid random access Rapid transfer rate
Floppy disc	Relatively small capacity Access – slower than Winchester, faster than cassette
Winchester disc drive	High capacity Swift access and transfer rates
Cassette	Very slow serial access Slow transfer rate

CHAPTER 3 QUESTIONS

1 Name two backing storage devices and state an application for each.
2 Give two examples of the use of ROM in a microcomputer. (S)
3 Why do computers require both ROM and RAM?
4 Distinguish between random and serial access storage. Use an example of each to illustrate your answer.
5 A wordprocessing package is too large for the whole of it to be held in main store at the same time as the document being processed. Explain how a backing store can be used for a program overlay in this case. (M)
6 Many users of microcomputers are upgrading their systems from tape cassette to floppy disc storage systems. What are the advantages of this operation?
7 State one advantage of bubble memory chips over standard RAM chips.
8 A large corporation is considering the use of videodiscs in its staff training programme. State one advantage and one disadvantage of this action.
9 State one application for which sequential access processing would be appropriate, and a second which would require direct access. Give two reasons to justify each application.

COMPUTER ARITHMETIC AND LOGIC

CONTENTS

Computers use **binary** arithmetic. **Only two states are permissible,** 0 and 1. This type of arithmetic is used not because it is impossible to build circuits which would operate in our normal (base 10) arithmetic, but because the potential for error is greatly reduced:

—   **a hole**, in punched card or paper tape, **exists (1) or it does not (0).**
—   **a dot**, on magnetic tape or disc, **is magnetised N–S or S–N.**
—   **a pulse of electric current**, in the CPU, **is large enough to represent 1 (5 volts) or it is not (0 volts).**
—   **a pulse of light transmitted** along a fibre optic cable **represents 1, its absence 0.**

BINARY SYSTEM

Like our ordinary base 10 (denary) system, this uses place value, but each place increases by a power of 2 rather than by a power of 10. Thus the columns are 'headed':

power of 2	2^7	2^6	2^5	2^4	2^3	2^2	2^1	2^0
denary equivalent	128	64	32	16	8	4	2	units

Example 1: Express 111011_2 as a denary number (notice the use of the small suffix '2' to indicate the base of the number).

Write down the binary number and over the top of each digit its column value:

```
32  16  8  4  2  u
 1   1  1  0  1  1
```

Hence: 111011_2 = (1*32) + (1*16) + (1*8) + (0*4) + (1*2) + 1 unit
= 32 + 16 + 8 + 2 + 1
= 59

Notice that '4' is omitted from the final calculation because there is a 0 in that column (0*4=0).

Now try question 1 at the end of this chapter.

To convert a denary number to binary the simplest method is to reverse this procedure.

Example 2: Express 78 as a binary number.
Method 1 Work out the highest power of 2 smaller than the given number – in this case $2^6=64$ – and write down the powers of 2 to this point as column headings, putting a 1 in the '64' column:

$$64 \quad 32 \quad 16 \quad 8 \quad 4 \quad 2 \, \text{unit}$$
$$ 1$$

Subtract 64 from 78 and repeat this process (subtracting the column value each time a '1' is inserted in a column) until the required number is represented.

$$64 \quad 32 \quad 16 \quad 8 \quad 4 \quad 2 \, \text{unit}$$
$$1 \quad 0 \quad 0 \quad 1 \quad 1 \quad 1 \quad 0$$

Hence: $78 = 1001110_2$

Check your answer using the method of Example 1.

Alternatively the 'remainder' method can be used:

Method 2 Set down a division sum and repeatedly divide by 2, making a note of the remainder on each line.

2)78	R 0
2)39	R 1
2)19	R 1
2)9	R 1
2)4	R 0
2)2	R 0
2)1	R 1
0	

The answer is obtained by reading the column of remainders upwards $78 = 1001110_2$.

Now try question 2 at the end of this chapter.

The complete set of **alphanumeric characters** – numbers and letters – as well as special characters, instruction and address codes are represented as unique combinations of 1s and 0s. Each 1 or 0 is called a bit (binary digit) and the number of bits required to represent a

Figure 4.1 ASCII Code – digits and letters

A	1000001	a	1100001	1	0110001
B	1000010	b	1100010	2	0110010
C	1000011	c	1100011	3	0110011
D	1000100	d	1100100	4	0110100
E	1000101	e	1100101	5	0110101
F	1000110	f	1100110	6	0110110
G	1000111	g	1100111	7	0110111
H	1001000	h	1101000	8	0111000
I	1001001	i	1101001	9	0111001
J	1001010	j	1101010	0	0110000
K	1001011	k	1101011		
L	1001100	l	1101100		
M	1001101	m	1101101		
N	1001110	n	1101110		
O	1001111	o	1101111		
P	1010000	p	1110000		
Q	1010001	q	1110001		
R	1010010	r	1110010		
S	1010011	s	1110011		
T	1010100	t	1110100		
U	1010101	u	1110101		
V	1010110	v	1110110		
W	1010111	w	1110111		
X	1011000	x	1111000		
Y	1011001	y	1111001		
Z	1011010	z	1111010		

single character is called a byte. The commonly used ASCII code (American Standard Code for Information Interchange) uses 7 bits for each character.

Computer processors operate in **multiples** of 8 bits; this is the word length of the computer – it is the number of bits which can be processed in a single operation. The eighth bit in each byte is used as a **parity** check, i.e. the most left-hand digit is used to make either an odd or an even number of 1s **in every character representation**. Using an even parity, the word BLUE would be encoded as:

01000010   B
11001100   L
01010101   U
11000101   E

The difficulty of checking the above coding will have given some indication of the difficulty of programming in machine code (see p.93) using pure binary representation. As a programming aid two other codes were quickly adopted – octal and hexadecimal.
Octal is base 8. $8 = 2^3$, therefore each octal digit can be converted to a group of 3 binary digits.

Example 3: Express 765_8 as a binary number

$$7 \quad 6 \quad 5$$
$$111 \quad 110 \quad 101$$

Hence $765_8 = 111110101_2$.
Hexadecimal (hex) is base 16. $16 = 2^4$. A similar process to find the binary equivalent is followed, but each hexadecimal digit is represented by 4 binary digits. In order to give the full single digit range in base 16 **the letters A to F are used to represent the values 10 to 15**.

Example 4: Express the hexadecimal number 1C9 in pure binary form.

$$1 \quad C \quad 9$$
$$0001 \quad 1100 \quad 1001$$

Hence $1C9_{hex} = (000)111001001_2$
       $1C9_{hex} = 111001001_2$

To convert from binary to octal (or hexadecimal) the reverse process is followed and the binary digits are grouped in 3s (or 4s) to give the individual octal (or hex) digits (see question 3 at the end of this chapter).

A further method of coding is **binary coded decimal (BCD)**. This code is used, as the name suggests, to convert directly from a denary number to a binary equivalent. Each of the digits 0 to 9 uses four digits (and 4 must be used) in its coded form.

Example 5: Express 473 in BCD

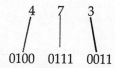

Hence 473 = 010001110011 in BCD.

To convert a number coded in BCD to its denary equivalent, the reverse procedure is followed, i.e. the numbers are grouped in 4s to give each denary digit.

Because binary representation is used for both numbers and characters the computer must be told which it is processing; the binary expression 01000001, for instance, could be the letter 'A' or the number 65. The convention for this distinction will depend upon the programming language – in BASIC the symbol '$' is used.

CODING

Two methods are commonly used to distinguish and encode positive and negative numbers:
(i)   **sign and magnitude**
(ii)   **two's complement**

SIGN AND MAGNITUDE

This coding uses the first (most significant) bit to indicate whether a number is positive (0) or negative (1). The remaining bits represent the size of the number in pure binary. So that:

$$01011011 = +91$$
sign bit
$$11011011 = -91$$

The major disadvantage of this coding is the use of two representations for zero. For instance, in an 8-bit word the numbers which can be represented range in size from 01111111 (+127) to 11111111 (−127) but, halfway between the two figures, both 00000000 and 10000000 represent zero.

TWO'S COMPLEMENT

This representation of positive numbers is identical to that of sign and magnitude, but in the coding of negative numbers the most significant bit has a negative value (rather than merely indicating the sign).

Example 7: The 8-bit binary number 11011011_2 is written in two's complement. State the denary number which it represents.

Write down the denary equivalent above the column of each digit.

128	64	32	16	8	4	2	U
1	1	0	1	1	0	1	1

negative   add

-128 $(64+16+8+2+1) = 91$

Therefore $11011011_2 = -128+91 = -37$.

In an 8-bit word the range of values is 01111111 (+127) to 10000000 (−128).

FORMING THE TWO'S COMPLEMENT

The easiest method of forming the two's complement representation of a negative number is to:

1   write the binary equivalent of the positive number (be sure to use the correct number of bits stated in the question);
2   change all the 0s to 1s and all the 1s to 0s;
3   add 1.

Example 8: Express −45 in two's complement using 8 bits.

1   45 =   00101101
2   Changing 1s and 0s   11010010
3   add 1   +1
Hence the two's complement is 11010011.
Check by using the method of Example 7:

11010011
$-128 + 83 = -45$

Although two's complement increases the range of number representation by 1 for a given number of bits, its main advantage is enabling all binary subtractions to be performed as if they were additions (i.e. the same circuits are used plus a NOT gate to reverse the digits).

Example 9: Calculate $11010_2 + 1011_2$

```
   11010
+   1011
--------
  100101
```

Therefore $11010_2 + 1011_2 = 100101_2$

Example 10: Calculate $23 - 9$ using two's complement and 8-bit representation.

The calculation is performed as $(-9)+23$. It is common to have a ninth overflow bit in these questions – as the check shows, it does NOT form a part of the answer.

First form the two's complement representation of -9

$$9 = 00001001$$
reverse the bits 11110110
add 1 $\quad 11110111$ $(-9$ in two's complement$)$
now add 23 $\quad 00010111$
$\overline{100001110}$

overflow bit

i.e. $23 - 9 = 00001110_2$

(Check the accuracy of this calculation by converting the answer to a denary value and **always** check in an examination to ensure that you have not made a simple slip.)

Example 11: Calculate $9 - 23$ using two's complement 8-bit representation add

$$-23 = 11110010 \text{ (in two's complement form)}$$
$$9 = 00001001$$
$$\overline{11110010}$$

The most significant '1' shows that the answer is **negative** (as you would expect). To find the equivalent denary value either form the two's complement of the answer or use the method of Example 7.
Using two's complement
reverse the digits giving 00001101
add 1 giving $\qquad\qquad 00001110$ (14)
Hence $9 - 23 = -14$.

LOGIC GATES

Inside the computer binary digits are represented by **electronic pulses**. **Logic gates**, the basic element of all digital electronic circuits, manipulate these pulses by opening or closing – allowing a pulse to pass (0) or not to pass (1) – according to their specified function. Logic gates are combined to produce logic circuits capable not only of **addition** but also the **comparison** of binary words (tests for equality or size) and **decoding**, i.e. the recognition of predetermined binary patterns.

The function of a logic gate is most easily understood using a **truth table** which shows all the possible combinations of pulses entering the gate and the output of the gate in each case.

The three most basic gates are:

1   the NOT gate which simply reverses (inverts) the incoming pulse;

Figure 4.2 NOT gate

Input (A)	Output (not A)
1	0
0	1

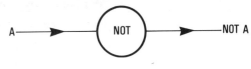

Note: It is common practice for examining groups to use circles and, as above, name the gate, but alternatively recognized symbols could be used for their identification. These are summarized in Figure 4.7.

2   the AND gate has at least two inputs but its output will only be 1 if **all** the inputs are 1;

Figure 4.3 The AND gate

A	B	C
0	0	0
0	1	0
1	0	0
1	1	1

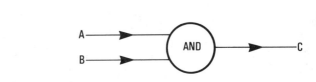

3   the OR gate also has at least two inputs but its output is 1 if **any** of the input pulses is 1.

Figure 4.4 The OR gate

A	B	C
0	0	0
0	1	1
1	0	1
1	1	1

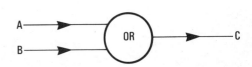

A knowledge of three other gates may also be required:

4   the NAND gate, which produces the opposite output to an AND gate (an AND gate followed by a NOT gate);

A	B	C
0	0	1
0	1	1
1	0	1
1	1	0

5 the **NOR** gate which produces the opposite output to an OR gate (an OR gate followed by a NOT gate);

A	B	C
0	0	1
0	1	0
1	0	0
1	1	0

6 the **EXCLUSIVE–OR** gate which will only give an output of 1 if the input pulses are different.

A	B	C
0	0	0
0	1	1
1	0	1
1	1	0

Example 12: Construct a truth table to show the outputs at P, Q, R and S in the diagram below.

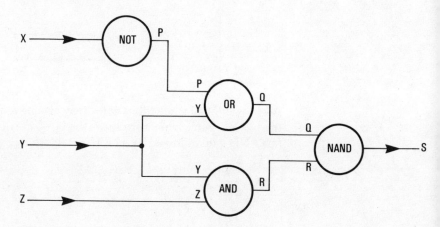

Figure 4.5 Combination gates

X	Y	Z	P	Q	R	S
0	0	0	1	1	0	1
0	0	1	1	1	0	1
0	1	0	1	1	0	1
0	1	1	1	1	1	0
1	0	0	0	0	0	1
1	0	1	0	0	0	1
1	1	0	0	1	0	1
1	1	1	0	1	1	0

Note: If the number of inputs to a system is 'n', then the total number of distinct combinations is 2^n. In this case the **3** inputs provide 8 ($=2^3$) combinations which are equivalent to the binary number patterns of 0 to 7.

Example 13: A safety system on a machine uses three switches A, B, C. The motor receives a stop signal X:

1 if switch A is closed (B and C being open); *or*
2 if switch C is closed (A and B being open); *or*
3 if A, B and C are all closed.

Draw a truth table showing all possible states of the switches and whether the motor is running or stopped. Also draw a logic network using AND, OR and NOT gates with A, B and C as inputs and the stop signal X as output.

A	B	C	X
0	0	0	0
0	0	1	1
0	1	0	0
0	1	1	0
1	0	0	1
1	0	1	0
1	1	0	0
1	1	1	1

The truth table is shown above. In the second row, for instance, switches A and B are open with switch C closed. This combination gives a stop signal, i.e. X=1.

The equivalent logic network is shown below. Notice that each of the AND gates has three inputs – you should trace each of these and confirm that the inputs correspond to the pattern in the truth table. The final OR gate enables any of the three conditions to supply the stop signal.

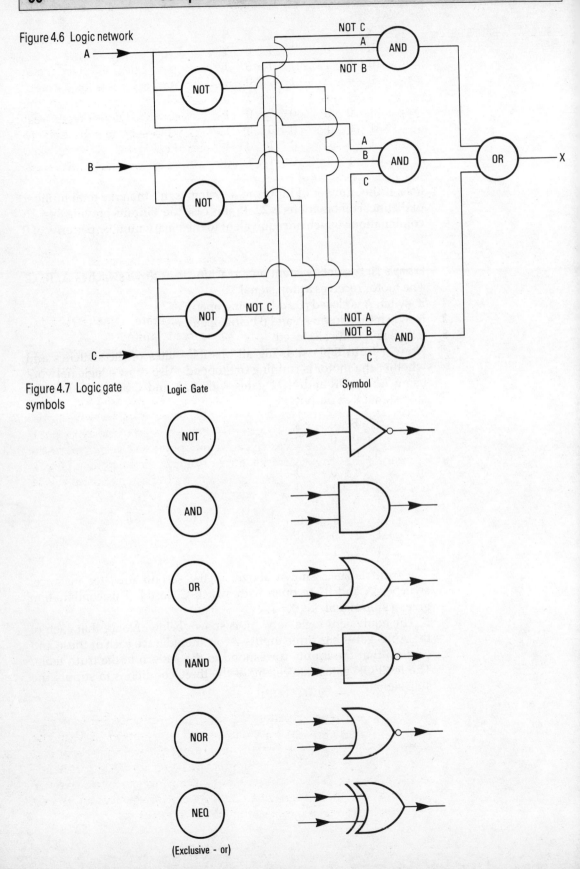

Figure 4.6 Logic network

Figure 4.7 Logic gate symbols

FIXED POINT AND FLOATING POINT ARITHMETIC

So far we have used only **integers** (whole numbers). We have made no reference to the **bicimal point** – the 'decimal point' of a binary number – because it has been in a **fixed position** immediately to the right of the least significant bit. To represent **non-integer real numbers** (fractions, decimals) the bicimal point must be able to occupy **different positions**. Whenever the bicimal point is **fixed somewhere** in the word(s) containing the number, **fixed point representation is being used**.

Example 14: Fixed point representation

$$10.5 \qquad\qquad\qquad\qquad = \quad 1010_{\uparrow}1$$

$$\text{The position of the bicimal point}$$

$$12.25 \qquad\qquad\qquad\qquad = 1100_{\uparrow}01$$

Fixed point representation is extremely accurate, but the range of possible numbers which can be represented is limited.

The alternative is to use **floating point representation**. In this case the bicimal point is always in the same position – normally immediately to the right of the sign bit. The representation contains not only the number – called the mantissa – but also an exponent which dictates the number of places which the bicimal must be moved from the representation to the correct position. The sign of the exponent is important. If it is positive (0) the bicimal point will be moved to the right; if it is negative (1) to the left. In Example 15 the bicimal point is shifted four places as it is floated to the front of the mantissa; this is, therefore, the value of the exponent.

Example 15: Floating point representation

$$13 = \qquad 01101 | 100$$

$$\text{mantissa} \qquad\quad \text{exponent}$$

Example 16:

$$23.5 \qquad = 10111_{\uparrow}1$$

its floating point representation is, therefore:

$$23.5 \quad = 0101111\ 0101$$

Floating point representation requires some balance between the number of bits used in the mantissa and the number used in the exponent. In practice the number of bits in the mantissa is expanded to give the required number of significant figures for the task at hand, so that floating point representations often occupy one-, two- or four-word lengths. The use of floating point representation greatly increases the range of possible number representations.

APPARENT ERRORS IN COMPUTER ARITHMETIC

Apparent errors arise because all computers have a **finite limit** for number representations. If a number is particularly large, small or represented by a recurring pattern, there will be insufficient bits for an exact representation.

OVERFLOW

Overflow occurs if the number is too large for the word(s) length allocated. The largest number which can be represented in 8 bits in fixed-point format is 127 (01111111); if the result of an arithmetic operation were to exceed this figure it would overflow and **the least significant bits would be lost**.

Example 17:

Express 116 and 27 in 16-bit words using 8 bits for each mantissa. Calculate 116+27 using the same representation and comment on the result.

$$116 = 0111010000000111$$
$$27 = 0110110000000101$$

For the calculation both exponents are made the same

$$116 = 0111010000000111$$
$$27 = 0001101100000111$$

Now add the mantissas (the exponents remain the same)

$$116+27 = 01000111100000111$$

Expressing this with 8 bits for the mantissa forces the least significant bit to be omitted, giving the answer:

$$0100011100001000$$

(The exponent is increased by one to allow for the shift of the number.)

This is the number 142, NOT the expected answer of 143. The error is caused by overflow.

UNDERFLOW

Underflow occurs when a number is too small for the word length.

TRUNCATION

When 'excess' figures are simply ignored the resulting error is called a **truncation** error. In fractional representation this error is reduced by **rounding**, i.e. the last digit is increased by 1 if the next figure would have been 1 (this is equivalent to an 8-digit calculator representing 2/3 as 0.6666667 rather than 0.6666666). The answer will still be inaccurate but the rounding error will be an improvement over simple truncation.

<table>
<tr><td>SUMMARY:</td><td>1</td><td>Computers use binary arithmetic – the two states can be represented in a variety of ways.</td></tr>
<tr><td></td><td>2</td><td>Alphanumeric characters, special characters, address and instruction codes are represented as unique combinations of 1s and 0s. The most common character code is the ASCII code.</td></tr>
<tr><td></td><td>3</td><td>Octal and hexadecimal codes were rapidly adopted to overcome the difficulty of programming in pure binary.</td></tr>
<tr><td></td><td>4</td><td>Numbers are coded using sign and magnitude or two's complement, with fixed or floating point notation.</td></tr>
<tr><td></td><td>5</td><td>Logic gates manipulate electronic pulses equivalent to the binary digits and are combined into logic circuits capable of arithmetic operations.</td></tr>
<tr><td></td><td>6</td><td>Apparent errors may arise in computer calculations due to:
(a)   overflow or underflow;
(b)   truncation or rounding.</td></tr>
</table>

CHAPTER 4 QUESTIONS

1 Express 1111010_2 as a decimal number.
2 Express 35 as a binary number.
3 Describe the different ways in which a binary code can be represented in computer applications.
4 If a computer has a six-bit word and the most significant bit is the sign bit, what is the largest positive number which can be represented
    (a)   in denary?
    (b)   in binary?   (L)
5 The number -23 is stored in 6 bits in two's complement form as

       101001

    (a)   complete the boxes with 1s and 0s to show how 27 would be stored.

       ☐☐☐☐☐☐

    (b)   complete the boxes with 1s and 0s to show how -27 would be stored

       ☐☐☐☐☐☐

                                        (N)
6 Express 27 and -27 in sign and magnitude form using 6 bits.

7 Express
   (a)   14
   (b)   15.5
   (c)   7.875
in fixed point and floating point representations. (Use 10 bits with 4 bits for the mantissa.) Comment.

8 What is meant by the terms 'underflow' and 'overflow'?

9 A microcomputer has an 8-bit word. Describe how this word length can be used to store characters and integers in two's complement form. State the range of integers which could be held and the number of characters.

10 Fill in the blank spaces in the table with 0 or 1 as appropriate, to represent the outputs P, Q and R for the given logic network.

Figure Ques 10

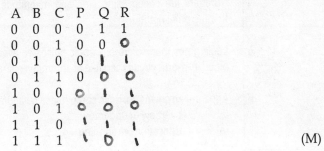

A	B	C	P	Q	R
0	0	0	0	1	1
0	0	1	0	0	0
0	1	0	0	1	1
0	1	1	0	0	0
1	0	0	0	1	1
1	0	1	0	0	0
1	1	0	1	1	1
1	1	1	1	0	1

(M)

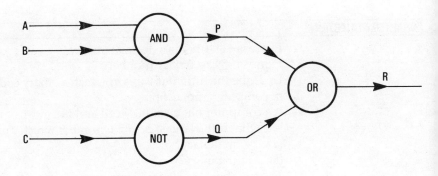

11   A water pump for a room
     heating system is to switch on if
     all the following conditions are
     fulfilled:

     (a)   The room is cold.
     (b)   Hot water is available.
     (c)   It is during the time set
           on the time switch or
           the manual override
           switch is set to 'on'.

Complete the section of truth
table shown alongside for this
situation using the codes:

R = 1   means room warm
         enough;
W = 1   means hot water is
         available;
T = 1   means set time for
         heating to be on;
M = 1   means manual override
         switch is set to 'on';
P = 1   means pump on.

Inputs				Output
R	W	T	M	P
0	0	1	0	0
0	0	1	1	0
0	1	0	0	0
0	1	0	1	1
0	1	1	0	1
0	1	1	1	1
1	0	1	1	0
1	1	0	0	0
1	1	1	0	0
1	1	1	1	0

(N)

DATA AND FILES

CONTENTS

The possible introduction of a computer processing system in a commercial, industrial or administrative situation should be preceded by two basic questions:

1 **What information is required from the system?**
2 **What information must be input to generate that specified output?**

The answers will determine not only **how** the input information will be encoded i.e. how the data will be structured and **what** processing (and hardware) will be required, but also **where** the input information will be collected.

If the introduction of a computer system is not given careful planning its implementation could not only be a failure – it could be disastrous, possibly leaving productivity lower than in the system which it replaced.

DATA CAPTURE

This is the collection of input information for computer processing. The particular application will determine the most efficient and appropriate method; some possibilities are:

(i) **a control process** which monitors variables with great frequency. This is automatic data collection – these analogue values will be converted to the digital equivalent and input directly to the computer.

(ii) **bar codes** which are increasingly used in the retail sector to gather sales information.

(iii) **traffic flow surveys** which may be made either manually or automatically.

(iv) **opinion** surveys such as political prediction polls, commercial product surveys etc.

(v) **official forms** such as driving licence applications, birth registration, taxation forms.

(vi) **data logging**, e.g. the logging of the variables in a scientific experiment at predetermined intervals over an extended period of time.

In some of these cases, such as bar codes, the information is already coded in a form suitable for input to the computer, but the vast majority of applications information is still obtained from handwritten forms. Modern forms can be precisely constructed to facilitate computer processing. They may contain:

(i) **simple** yes/no responses to questions;

(ii) **one choice** from a variety of options;

(iii) **standardized formats** for any additional information.

Figure 5.1 Tutor group
questionnaire

> **TUTOR GROUP QUESTIONNAIRE**
>
> 1. Please state your age. Use each of the six boxes.
>
>   Example. 7th March 1976 = | 0 | 7 | 0 | 3 | 7 | 6 |
>
> | | | | | | |
>
> 2. Which Tutor Group are you in? | | | |
>
> 3. What is your sex   M/F | |
>
> 4. Are you late to school   never ☐
>   sometimes ☐
>   *Please tick only one box*   regularly ☐
>   always ☐

The information on such forms is input **directly** to the computer using optical character readers or mark sense readers, but many forms still permit the responses to be presented in a number of ways; for example, the question, 'Please state your date of birth' may give rise to any of the following responses: 16.03.86; 16 3 86; 16th. March 86; 16th March 1986; sixteenth March 1986.

DATA PREPARATION

Computers cannot cope with information presented in a variety of ways. Data preparation is the encoding of information in standard formats on a medium suitable for data processing. Codes are a common feature of our everyday lives:

— **product codes** e.g. paint codes, identify the product size, colour, type.

— **postal codes** locate very small areas of the country and ensure correct delivery.

— **car number plates** code the area and year of registration.

— **home shopping catalogues** give each item a different code – and each option on the item generates a different item code.

Encoding information for data processing makes it **concise, unambiguous** and **standardized**; each part of a code represents the same information, e.g. in a postal code the first letter(s) always represent

Figure 5.2 Postal code

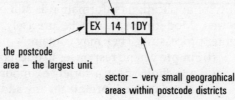

postcode district – a subdivision of the postcode area

| EX | 14 | 1DY |

the postcode area – the largest unit

sector – very small geographical areas within postcode districts

one of the 120 postcode areas into which the British Isles is divided. This is the structure of the data.

Data, **by itself**, is meaningless. The data 'TT 4 4.45', for instance, imparts no information until it is explained that it refers to a cross-channel ferry operator, stating the number of daily sailings and the average journey time in hours.

Data which has been processed into a meaningful form is information.

Data, with meaning, provides information.

We have already seen (p.58) that the most common code for representing the range of alphanumeric characters is the ASCII code. Using this, or a similar code, each digit or letter of the data must now be transcribed on to the medium to be used for the computer processing. Traditionally this required a punch operator to punch holes in cards or paper tape (see page 23), but keyboard input with storage on magnetic tape (key-to-tape) or magnetic disc (key-to-disc) is now almost universal.

VERIFICATION AND VALIDATION

Verification is the off-line process of confirming that data is **correct before** it is input to the computer. Punched cards were verified by 're-punching' the card in a verifier which would not actually punch any holes but would confirm that, were it to do so, they would be identical to those already punched. Similarly, paper tape was verified by producing a second tape of the same data and comparing the two tapes frame by frame. With direct data entry, using key-to-disc or key-to-tape, data is verified either by a series of prompts (on the VDU screen) requiring confirmation that the entry is correct or, much more rarely, by re-typing. The entries could be confirmed either by a second person reading the VDU screen or by the original operator, depending on company policy.

In some data preparation applications such as the Driving and Vehicle Licensing Centre at Swansea, data is prepared to standard formats. In this case the operator selects software appropriate to the particular data, which then determines the screen layout and confirms that certain responses contain the correct number of characters.

Validation processes are designed to check that the data is **accurate, believable** and **complete**. Validation is carried out by the computer (on line) at the input stage, either as a completely separate program or, for more limited applications, as a subroutine prior to the main processing.

Typical validation procedures are:

(*a*)   **Range checks** – to ensure that the data item lies within acceptable limits, e.g. the age of someone holding a motorcycling licence cannot be less than 16 and is unlikely to be more than 100!!

(*b*)   **Hash totals** – formed by adding together a series of data items (usually referring to one record). During the validation procedure the

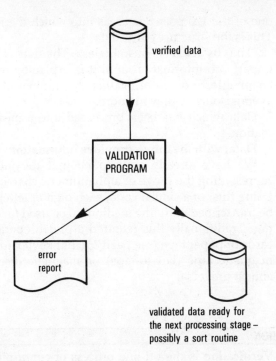

verified data

VALIDATION PROGRAM

error report

validated data ready for the next processing stage – possibly a sort routine

Figure 5.3 Data validation

computer repeats this calculation and compares its total with the hash total. Any discrepancy indicates an input error.

(*c*)   **Control totals** – formed in a similar way. They are the result of adding the data items of a specific field (or fields) in each group of records, or complete file, being run. This total provides sensible information, whereas a hash total will normally be a meaningless value which is used solely for checking purposes.

(*d*)   **Check digits** – frequently used in applications where a reference number identifies the customer, e.g. billing or rating systems. The check digit is calculated from the digits of the input number and 'added' to the end of that number.

The most common technique is to 'weight' each of the digits of the input number differentially; this will prevent:

1   **transcription errors** – the incorrect transfer of a number, e.g. keying a '2' instead of a '7'.
2   **transposition errors** i.e. the typing of two digits of a number in the wrong order. The number 23176 for instance could accidentally be keyed as 23716. This is a common error.

The calculation of check digits by the **weighted modulo 11 method** is particularly popular.

Example: Calculate the check digit for the input number 23176 using the weighted modulo 11 method.

First, each of the digits is given a different weighting factor, beginning with '2' in the units column.

The corresponding products are then calculated.

number   2   3   1   7   6

                 ×   ×   ×   ×   ×

weighting factor   6   5   4   3   2

                 ‖   ‖   ‖   ‖   ‖

product   12   15   4   21   12

    total $(12+15+4+21+12) = 64$.

The remainder after dividing by 11 is 9; subtract this figure from 11 $(11-9) = 2$

This figure is the check digit and it completes the input number which would now be:

    2   3   1   7   6   2

The final figure now generated by the weighted modulo check is divisible by 11. **During processing the calculation will be repeated** and the divisibility checked to confirm that there is no error in data entry. Similarly, if a more sophisticated check digit calculation is used, the check digit is always recalculated during processing and compared with the original.

The ISBN number of this book contains a final check digit calculated in precisely this way – confirm for yourself that the weighted total which it generates is divisible by 11. All ISBN numbers contain this check digit and are checked automatically during any computer process such as re-ordering.

Other possible validation checks include **parity checks** (see p.59), **invalid character checks** and **consistency checks**. The latter compare the data items of a single record with each other to ensure that they provide compatible information.

DATA FILES

Data is normally organized into files. A **file** is an organized collection of related records which share a common structure.

Every data item forms a **field** (but with some fixed length field applications it may not use all the available bits); this is the smallest subdivision of the data, e.g. Christian name, surname, age, sex. **The fields which relate to one person or product are grouped together to form a record**. The set of records forms a file.

Example:

1   The file of driving licence information is kept by the Driver and Vehicle Licensing Centre (DVLC).

2 The file is divided into records which provide the full information about any one driver.

3 Each driver's record is divided into fields with each field holding a single piece of information, e.g. his name, his address.

The complete system can be compared with a traditional card filing system which uses a separate card for each record. The entries on the cards correspond to fields and the set of cards forms a file.

Figure 5.4 Filing cabinet

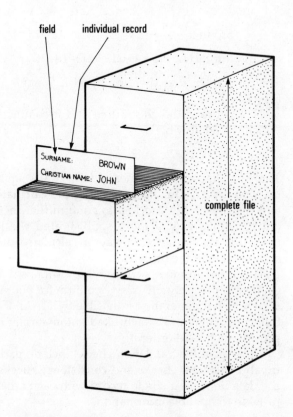

By encoding the data many of the fields will have a fixed length, e.g. the standard use of M or F for a person's sex. If this is not the case and variable field lengths are used, special characters are needed as end-of-field and end-of-record markers.

KEY FIELDS

So that any record can be 'picked out' from a file it is necessary to have one particular field which identifies the record uniquely. This is called the key and it must appear in the **same place in each record** of the file. Name fields are not unique and, therefore, should not be used as the key. Suitable key fields are individual code numbers, e.g. account numbers, employee numbers, ISBN book numbers.

The first record of a file often has a special purpose – it is the header containing information about the file: its name, the total number of records and possibly the date of its construction. If the file is sequential (see below), the header will usually be followed by the index, i.e. a list of the keys. Similarly, the final record will often contain only an end-of-file marker.

SERIAL, SEQUENTIAL AND DIRECT ACCESS FILES

In a **serial file** no attempt is made to relate the position of one record with another. There is no logical alphabetic or numerical progression. Data is normally stored in this way only for short periods, such as when a **transaction file** is being created (see p.84).

Sequential files, as the name suggests, are arranged in a logical sequence – **the order of their keys**. This organization enables a specified record to be located much more quickly and it is essential for efficient file handling processes such as updating and merging. An indexed sequential file reduces access time still further by searching the index, rather than the file, to establish the position of a specific record.

The address of **random (also called direct) access files** is determined by an algorithm based on the key of the file. The same algorithm is used both to generate the address and to retrieve the file from that address. It is possible, therefore, to move directly to that position without reading the contents of other files.

Note:

(i) **Magnetic tape** is a serial access medium. It is most efficient when storing serial or sequential files and particularly appropriate for storing very large amounts of data which is rarely accessed, e.g. security copies, or for batch processing applications in which every record is read and its data routinely processed e.g. payroll systems.

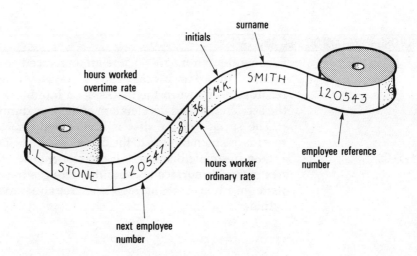

Figure 5.5   Sequential payroll records on magnetic tape

(ii) **Magnetic discs** (including Winchesters and floppy discs) are direct access storage mediums – the time to reach any address is independent of its location. This medium is ideal for random access files, which are the most appropriate in applications which may demand frequent, rapid and unpredictable access to information, e.g. bank accounts. Customer enquiries are unpredictable and require immediate response.

Figure 5.6 Bank account enquiry

It should not be assumed that magnetic discs are used solely for direct access files; **indexed sequential files** which can be directly or sequentially accessed are used extensively.

FILE ORGANIZATION ON DISC AND TAPE

Files written on magnetic tape are organized so that the records are grouped into **data blocks**. Each block may consist of one or more records and between the blocks is an **interblock gap**; this allows for the acceleration and deceleration of the tape during processing.

The surface of the **disc** is divided into **tracks** and **sectors**. The records are then written to the disc as shown below.

In a magnetic disc pack, if the storage exceeds a single track the next available **surface** is used; this reduces travel time for the read/write head in both storage and retrieval and creates a **storage cylinder**.

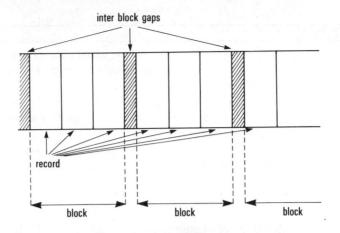

Figure 5.7 File organization on magnetic tape

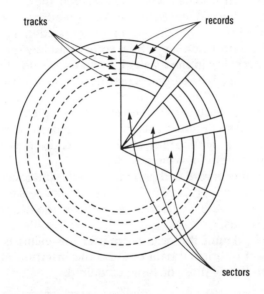

Figure 5.8 File organization on magnetic disc

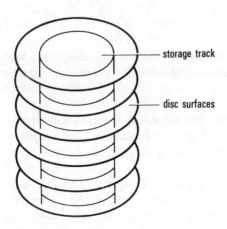

Figure 5.8A A storage cylinder

FILE MANAGEMENT

Three types of file – called file generations – are identified:

(*a*)   **The master file**, which is the principal store of data for that application.

(*b*)   **The transaction file**, which contains the most recent application data. It is used to update the master file at intervals determined by the application.

(*c*)   The process of updating the existing master file with the transaction file creates a new master file – this is called **the son file**.

FILE UPDATING

Sequential master files are updated using a **batch processing system** which updates all the file records in a single operation. The interval between updates will depend upon the particular application. The following sequence describes the updating process:

1   If necessary, the contents of the transaction file are **validated**.

2   The transaction file is then **sorted into key order**, which ensures that the records in the master file and transaction file are read in the same sequence. The sorting is performed by a **utility** program (see p.100).

3   The key of the first transaction file is read and noted.

4   The master file is read through and **copied** to a new output file until that key is found. The master file record is then amended, with the contents of the transaction file and the new version written to the new output file – the son file.

5   Another record is then read from the transaction file and the process continued. The key order makes it unnecessary to read the master file from the start again; it can be examined from the current position onwards.

   Updating the original master file includes not only the amendment of original data but also the **insertion** of new records and the **deletion** of those no longer required.

FILE MERGING

The process of combining two files is called **merging**. The updating of a master file is a specific example. In general both files are sorted into key order and, at each stage, their next record key numbers compared; the record with the lowest key number is then copied to the output file.

On line systems use **direct access master files** to which changes are made at the time of processing. An update program **searches** – the process of finding a single record – the master file for the key of the record which is being processed (for instance the account number of a person using a bank cashpoint) and the master file is amended with the transaction details. For security purposes the updating process also produces a copy of all the transactions – the transaction file.

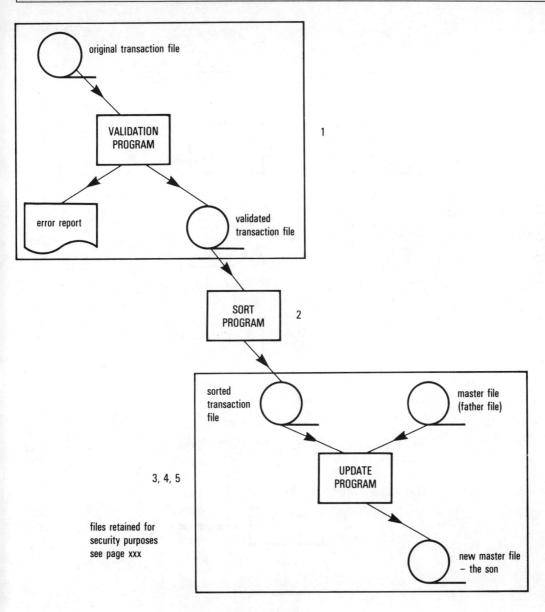

Figure 5.9 Updating sequential files

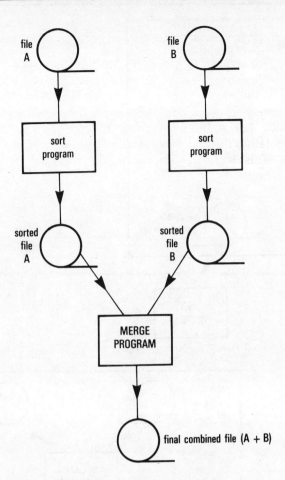

Figure 5.10 Merging two files

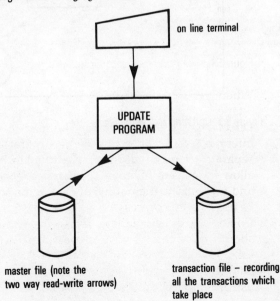

Figure 5.11 Updating
direct access files

FILE SECURITY

1 For sequential files copies of the master file, transaction file and son file should be kept, as shown in Figure 5.9. This will allow the son file – the most recent – to be regenerated should the need arise, i.e. the loss or corruption (errors in the data) of the son file in use.

For additional security the previous generation, i.e. the grandfather file and the preceding transaction file, should also be retained. This technique is called the **ancestral** or **grandfather-father-son** method of file security.

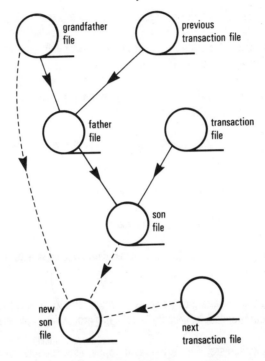

Figure 5.12 The ancestral system of file security

When the son file is updated it becomes the new father and, in a 3-tape system, the grandfather will become the new son.

2 Direct access files should be 'dumped' to magnetic tape at regular intervals and a transaction file incorporated in the system to keep a separate record of all the transactions in between. This, again, will allow the master file to be regenerated. (*Note*: magnetic tape is cheap and will hold vast amounts of data, but a second magnetic disc could be used for this process.)

3 Copies of magnetic tape or disc being retained for security purposes should be kept in the safest possible place – preferably a fireproof safe. the loss or corruption of computer files could be extremely damaging to commercial or industrial enterprises making extensive use of computer processing.

SUMMARY:		
	1	The introduction of any computer system requires careful planning.
	2	Data can be captured in a variety of ways depending on the particular application, but the majority is still collected on written forms.
	3	The encoding of data makes it concise, unambiguous and standardized.
	4	Data which has been processed into a meaningful form is information. Data alone is meaningless.
	5	Verification is an off-line process which confirms that the keyed data is correct.
	6	Validation processes are normally carried out by the computer and check that the data is accurate, believable and complete.
	7	Data is organized into files; a file is an organized collection of related records sharing a common structure.
	8	The smallest subdivision of a file is a field; the fields which relate to one person or product form a record.
	9	The key field uniquely identifies the record.
	10	A sequential file is arranged in the order of its keys.
	11	In a random access file, the address of each record is determined by an algorithm based on the key.
	12	Magnetic tape is a serial access medium and most efficient when used to store large amounts of data for security, or for batch processing applications, e.g. payroll systems.
	13	Magnetic discs, Winchesters and floppy discs support random access files which are most appropriate in applications demanding rapid, frequent and unpredictable access, e.g. customer enquiries.
	14	The master file is the principal store of data for a particular application. At intervals it is updated by a transaction file, holding the most recent data, to form the son file.
	15	Two files can be merged to form a single file.
	16	Data files are protected using the ancestral system of file security.

1   Describe a suitable method of data capture for a supermarket POS system.

2   What is the purpose of encoding data? State two codes with which you are familiar and describe what they contain.

3   How are data and information related?

4   What is the purpose of data validation? Describe three possible validation checks and suggest one item of data which might successfully pass these checks but still be invalid.

5   What is a check digit? Describe one application in which check digits are used.

6   Describe the relationship of the terms record, file and field.

7   Personnel records in a large company are held on a computer file on disc and are processed by the computer. The key field in each record contains the employees payroll number.

   (*a*)   What is a record?

   (*b*)   What is the key field?

   (*c*)   Give examples of cases where a record would need to be
   (i) deleted;
   (ii) inserted;
   (iii) amended.

   (*d*)   State, giving your reasons, which method would be used to access the file to find details of just one employee whose payroll number was known.   (W)

8   Describe the distinction between serial, sequential and direct access files. State a possible application for each.

9   Describe the process of updating a master file in
   (*a*)   a batch processing system holding the files on magnetic tape;
   (*b*)   a direct access application.

10   Describe three possible methods of file security.

11   When stock arrives at a warehouse, items which have not previously been held in stock are given new code numbers and new records and are then added to the stock file.

   The stock is held in order of code number.

   Explain the use of SORT and MERGE routines to do this.
                                                          (M)

COMMUNICATION WITH THE COMPUTER

CONTENTS

Computers can be distinguished from other calculating aids by their ability to execute a **stored** program, i.e. a sequence of statements designed to solve a specific problem. The storage of the program in the main memory enables the computer to work, **uninterrupted, at electronic speeds.** This facility and the compactness of electronic components provides high-speed data processing.

MACHINE CODE

Computers use only **binary numbers** (see chapter 4). A program written in pure binary is a machine code program – each program statement consists solely of a series of 1s and 0s. a machine code program breaks down each process or calculation into a series of very small steps and every step must provide the computer with **two** items of information:

    (1) **an instruction** – the operation code;

    (2) **a store location** inside the computer containing the value to be operated on – the memory address or operand.

For instance, to add together two numbers in locations 120 and 121 and store the result in location 122, a machine code program would specify the following steps:

    01   load the contents of store 120 into the accumulator
    02   add the contents of store 121 to the accumulator
    03   store the contents of the accumulator in location 122

The accumulator is a special register used for holding the current processing value or for data transfer.

In the program statements above both the **operation codes** and the **addresses** would be binary numbers. So that, in a computer which uses 8 bits for both the operation code and the operand, the series of instructions above may read:

    01   00000001 01111000
    02   00000010 01111001
    03   00000100 01111010

In this example there are 256 possible operation codes (8 bits provides $2^8 = 256$ numbers) and 256 possible addresses. The operation codes not only provide for **arithmetic functions** but also for **logical decisions** (is A greater than B) and for data transfer.

Some larger computers have a **second address**. This reduces the number of separate program statements and makes the machine code program much shorter. The three steps above, for instance, could have been represented in a single instruction:

00000010 01111000 01111001
add   A (and) B

THE FETCH-EXECUTE CYCLE

When a program is running each statement in turn is taken from the immediate access store, decoded by the CPU and executed. This, simply described, is the fetch-execute cycle.

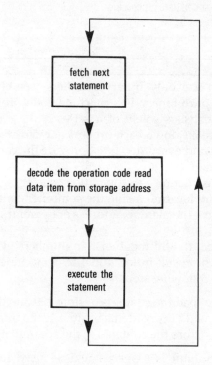

fetch next
statement

decode the operation code read
data item from storage address

execute the
statement

Figure 6.1 Simplified fetch-execute cycle

THE CHARACTERISTICS OF MACHINE CODE

1 Machine code is **orientated to the computer**. It is extremely laborious to program in machine code and programs are difficult to decode and modify.

2 Because each computer has its own set of operation codes, **machine code is not portable**, i.e. it cannot be easily transferred from one computer to another.

3 Machine code instructions are **executed more rapidly than any other programming source**, i.e. machine code programs are the fastest to run.

The difficulty of programming in machine code quickly led to the introduction of **hexadecimal** or **octal** bases (see p.59) to replace pure binary representation, and to the use of **mnemonics**. A mnemonic is a group of characters which represent a single operation code; the characters are chosen so that they 'suggest' the operation code which they represent. Mnemonics vary but characteristic examples (based on the 6502 microprocessor instruction set) are:

ADC   add the data item in a specified memory location to the accumulator;

LDA   load a data item in memory into the accumulator;

STA   store the accumulator contents in a specified memory location;

BPL   branch if the result of a calculation is positive;

JMP   jump to a new location;

PNT   output the contents of the accumulator.

Assembly language also permits the programmer to replace the **absolute** memory address with a set of characters – **a symbolic address**, e.g. LDA NUM1 would load the contents of the memory address NUM1 into the accumulator.

A program to add together two numbers in memory addresses NUM1 and NUM2 using assembly language would appear as:

```
01   LDA   NUM1
02   ADC   NUM2
03   STA   C
```

These statements have a **one-to-one correspondence** with the machine code program for the same calculation and show that assembly language is a programming tool **directly related** to individual computer design.

BRANCHING

A branching point in a program allows **control to be transferred** to another point in the program either:

(*a*)   **if a specified condition is satisfied**; or

(*b*)   **unconditionally**.

In the program below line 03 transfers control to program step 06 if the result of the addition in the first two lines is positive. If the result

```
01   LDA   28
02   ADC   29
03   BPL   02
04   STA   30
05   JMP   07
06   STA   40
07   END
```

is negative (i.e. the 'larger' of the two numbers stored in locations 28 and 29 is negative), branching does not take place and the result is stored in location 30. The branching instruction may **either** include the number of program steps to be omitted, as above where two programming steps are omitted, **or** stipulate the line to which control will be transferred. The latter possibility is shown in the program below:

```
01          LDA   28
02          ADC   29
03          BPL   POS
04          STA   30
05          JMP   07
06   POS    STA   40
07          END
```

Control would be transferred to the line labelled 'POS'. POS is called the **label**.

Line 05 is an unconditional transfer of control within the program.

Example 1: State the contents of the accumulator and memories as each instruction of the assembly language program below is executed. (This process, working through a program by hand, is called dry running.) Explain the purpose of the program.

The contents of memory locations NL1 and NW1 are 15 and 12 respectively.

```
01   LDA   NL1
02   ADC   NL1
03   STA   TP1
04   LDA   NW1
05   ADC   NW1
06   ADC   TP1
07   PNT
```

The solution below shows the store contents alongside the program steps. Try the question yourself before reading the answer.

			Accumulator	NL1	NW1	TP1
			0	15	12	0
01	LDA	NL1	15	15	12	0
02	ADC	NL1	30	15	12	0
03	STA	TP1	30	15	12	30
04	LDA	NW1	12	15	12	30
05	ADC	NW1	24	15	12	30
06	ADC	TP1	54	15	12	30
07	PNT					

OUTPUT 54

Notice that the contents of only **one** memory location change with each instruction.

The purpose of this program is to find the perimeter of a rectangle given its length and width.

ASSEMBLERS

Before an assembly language program can be executed it must first be translated to machine code. This process is performed by an **assembler** which:

(*a*)   converts mnemonic codes into machine language operational codes;

(*b*)   converts the symbolic addresses into absolute (actual) memory addresses; and

(*c*)   checks and reports any errors.

The assembly language program is called the **source code** and the final, error-free, version in machine language is the **object code**. The object code will then be run on the computer.

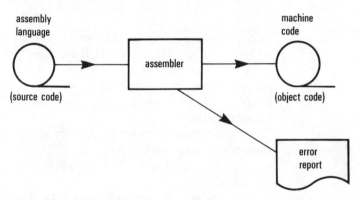

Figure 6.2 Assembly process

In addition to programming statements the assembly language (source code) program may also contain instructions to the assembler – called **directives** – which are not translated into the object code, e.g. END may tell the assembler that the program is now complete.

CHARACTERISTICS OF ASSEMBLY LANGUAGE

1   One-to-one correspondence with machine code.

2   Related to individual computer operational codes and therefore not readily portable between computers.

3   The use of mnemonics makes the programming much easier than in machine code.

4   Assembly language programs contain directives, which are not translated into the machine code version.

A further stage of assembly language development was the use of **autocodes** which allowed the program to 'call' a frequently used set of program instructions using one command. The assembler would then search for the required set of program instructions on permanently connected magnetic discs, and incorporate them into the object code. A set of instructions performing a specific task within the program, but which is not itself a complete program, is a **subroutine**.

Assembly language and machine code are **low-level languages**.

HIGH-LEVEL LANGUAGES

High-level languages are **user or problem orientated** rather than machine orientated. They consist of a series of **command words**, each of which may be equivalent to a number of program statements in machine code. In BASIC, for instance, the addition of two numbers in different storage locations and placement of the answer in a third location requires only one program step:

$$A = B+C$$

The programmer does not need to know the actual memory addresses or to be familiar with the machine architecture.

In addition, the computer systems which support high-level languages normally provide an extensive range of **diagnostic aids** to facilitate the identification and correction of programming errors. These may include:

(*a*)   **diagnostic error messages**, which pin-point the fault and the reason why it has occurred;

(*b*)   **trace routines**, which display each line number as it is executed;

(*c*)   **variable listing facilities** which display the variable values at strategic points in the program or, as an extension to the trace routine, display the variables at each program step.

CHARACTERISTICS OF HIGH-LEVEL LANGUAGES

1   Programming is a great deal easier. The program statements are similar to English phrases and are built from an extensive language vocabulary of command words and symbols.

2   Each high-level instruction is equivalent to a number of program steps in machine code (one-to-many correspondence).

3   There are a large number of high-level languages; some have been designed for a specific range of tasks, others are general purpose.

4   High-level languages are intended to be **portable** (machine independent). In practice, however, portability is restricted by:

(i)   **the dialect of the language.** High-level language development has not been static and enhanced versions of certain languages, notably BASIC, have been released at periodic intervals. Software written using recent versions may not run on all computers which support that language;

(ii)   limitations of **the operating system**;

(iii) **memory limitations** of the system.

SOME HIGH-LEVEL LANGUAGES AND THEIR APPLICATIONS

The first three high-level languages were developed during the late 1950s and early 1960s. Computers at that time were **very large, unreliable** and **extremely expensive**. Development was the result of government, military and, to a lesser extent, business sponsorship. These facts are reflected in their intended applications:

FORTRAN (FORmula TRANslation) is used extensively for science research applications. It manipulates numbers very accurately but has relatively poor string-handling and file-handling capabilities.

ALGOL (ALGOrithmic Language) was biased towards mathematical applications but could also be used in general purpose applications. The structured approach which it demands is of particular value.

COBOL (Common Business Orientated Language) is used in business and commercial applications. It offers good file-handling and string-handling features but only limited numerical facilities.

Despite their age both FORTRAN and COBOL are still used extensively. This is partially the result of **inertia**; once a language is firmly established the volume of **applications software** which it has generated ensures its continued use, though possibly in various versions. ALGOL has proved less popular, but the structured educational language PASCAL owes much to its development.

BASIC (Beginners All-purpose Symbolic Instruction Code) Originally designed as a simple introductory all-purpose language, it has now become the language of microcomputers. The lack of standardization of its various dialects is a significant problem but, nevertheless, it is widely used in education.

ADA has been developed by the United States Department of Defense. It is a complex language destined to be central in the control of the next generation of American missiles.

PROLOG is a language capable of making logical deductions from data premises. It has been adopted by the Japanese as the language for their fifth-generation computers.

LISP (LISt Processing) processes data in the form of lists. It is a complex language, used largely in artificial intelligence, and is the basis of LOGO – the naturally structured, graphics-orientated language used increasingly in primary schools.

FORTH is specifically designed for control applications and allows users to formulate new instructions from existing commands.

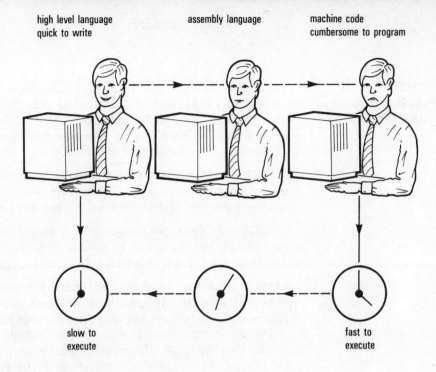

high level language
quick to write

assembly language

machine code
cumbersome to program

slow to
execute

fast to
execute

Figure 6.3 Summary diagram

AUTHOR LANGUAGES

These represent a further level in the hierarchy of programming languages; their program instructions closely resemble ordinary English statements. These languages, for instance PILOT and MICRO-TEXT, are of particular value in **CAL (computer assisted learning)** and in the development of **expert systems** (see next section) by allowing 'teachers' with little or no computing experience to write effective software.

UTILITY PACKAGES

Many **utility programs** (also called **library routines**) are supplied by the manufacturer as a part of the **systems software** – software which controls the performance of the computer system. They perform common but **important** tasks such as:

> **copying files**;
> **transferring data from one storage medium to another**; and
> **trace routines**.

Some utilities are sold separately to enhance those computer systems with a frequent need for their purpose. These may include:

> **sort routines**;
> **screen dump routines**; and

toolkit utilities designed to assist the programmer in debugging – the identification and removal of errors in a program.

The use of library programs saves time for the programmer and decreases the execution time, since many of the routines are written in machine code. In addition, they need not be in the memory until required.

APPLICATIONS PACKAGES

An applications package is the software (or firmware) which actually **puts the computer to work** on the task defined by the customer. Such packages are now available 'off-the-shelf' for a wide range of commercial applications based on microcomputer and minicomputer specifications. They include general purpose programs, e.g. word processors, spreadsheets and specific business software such as company payroll systems and vehicle scheduling systems. These packages are relatively cheap and, therefore, appropriate to small company applications. An off-the-shelf package may not fit the exact task definition, but its **user friendliness**, **versatility** and **flexibility** should allow the customer to tailor it to his own requirements. The ideal package will also be **robust**, **reliable** and **portable**.

Large institutions using mainframe computers, such as the clearing banks and large insurance companies, will normally write their own applications software.

One special type of applications package is the **expert system**. In this type of package expert(s) impart their experience and knowledge into a computer system which then enables a person of more limited experience to reach expert conclusions. Expert systems have, for instance, been developed for medical diagnosis and geological applications. Such systems have yet to achieve the popularity envisaged by the Alvey Report and doubts are increasingly being expressed. The decision-making process of any expert program is not infallible and the problem of **legal responsibility** is crucial. In addition, the ability of expert systems to **explain their conclusions** to the user is being called into question.

INTERPRETERS AND COMPILERS

High-level languages cannot be immediately executed by the computer; they must first be translated into machine code. Two methods are available:

(*a*)   **The compiler** translates **all** the original program (source code) into the machine program (object code) in **one operation**. It is not interrupted by errors – a complete list is given at the end of the compilation. These are then corrected and the **whole program must be re-compiled**. In an error-free program, compilation takes place only **once**.

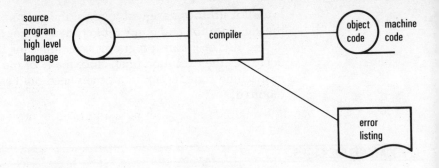

Figure 6.4 Compilation

(b)　　**The interpreter translates** and **executes** the source code **line-by-line**; any error found interrupts the execution of the program, but can be quickly dealt with and the program run again. Each time the program is run, **it must be re-interpreted**.

Figure 6.5 Interpretation

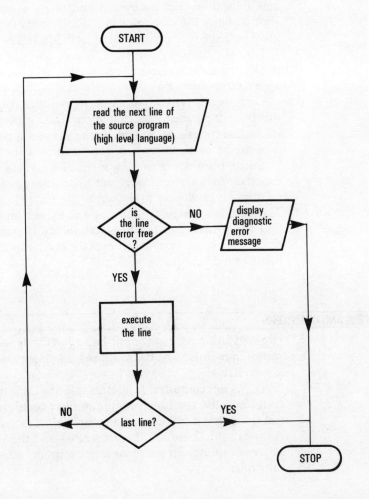

Although the process of compilation requires substantial memory space since the source code, object code and compiler must be stored simultaneously, and is relatively slow, the resultant object code is executed much more rapidly than an interpreted source code. The selection of one method in preference to the other may well depend on:

1 **the system.** Some larger mini and mainframe systems use only compilation.
2 **the number of times the program is expected to be run.** If this number is significantly large, then a compiled program in machine code would be advantageous.
3 **the language.** Some high-level languages are not available with interpreters.

Since every computer is ultimately run by a set of machine code instructions, one recent line of development has been to **reduce** the core of operations in this instruction set. This is called RISC (reduced instruction set computer) technology and it will enable computers to run faster and more efficiently.

ERRORS

Syntax errors (or **compilation errors**) occur when the rules of the language are broken, e.g. INPIT in mistake for INPUT. Syntax errors are detected during compilation or interpretation and the computer system displays a diagnostic error message to indicate the type of error and its location. A typical example from a BASIC interpreter is:

SYNTAX ERROR   LINE 30

Some errors such as **underflow** and **overflow** (see p.68) will only be detected during program execution. They are called **run-time** or **execution errors**. A calculation which eventually leads to division by zero is a common example. Again, most computer systems will provide a diagnostic error message; for instance:

e.g. Division by zero at line 1540

is displayed in BASIC on reaching a calculation which divides by zero.

The computer system cannot identify incorrect results given by a **logical error** in the design of the program. **Test data**, for which the expected results are specified and which will test the program for all possible circumstances, should always be used to thoroughly check a program. **A dry run** may also be used in conjunction with test data to confirm that the program is correct **before it is run** or to **locate** the logic error if the program is found to be incorrect.

SUMMARY:

1 A machine code program is written in binary code. It is the fastest type of program to execute, but machine orientated and extremely cumbersome to program.

2 The accumulator is a special register used to hold the current processing value or for data transfer.

3 Each machine code instruction contains an operation code and a store location which holds the data to be operated on.

4 The fetch-execute cycle is the process of taking each program instruction in turn from memory, decoding and executing it.

5 Assembly language uses mnemonic codes to simplify the programmers' task.

6 Each program statement in assembly language has one-to-one correspondence with machine code.

7 A branching point allows control to be transferred to another point in the program. The transfer may be either conditional or unconditional.

8 Dry running is the process of working through program statements by hand.

9 Assembly language programs are translated to machine code by an assembler before being executed.

10 High-level program languages are user or problem orientated rather than machine orientated. Programming statements use command words and symbols from an extensive vocabulary and resemble English phrases. Each program step may be equivalent to several steps in machine code.

11 Different dialects of a high-level language will restrict its portability.

12 There are a large variety of high-level languages.

13 Utility programs perform common but important tasks, e.g. copying files, transferring data.

14 The use of library programs saves programming and execution time.

15 Compilers translate a complete high-level program to machine code in a single operation and, thereafter, the compiled version is run. An interpreter performs the same task line by line-executing each line as it is translated.

16 Syntax and run-time errors are identified by the computer system which then displays a diagnostic error message. Logical errors can only be identified by comparison of the computer output with known results.

1   Briefly describe the fetch-execute cycle and the structure of a machine code instruction.

2   State the characteristics of machine code. Use this text to find out whether it is an applications or a systems programmer who will normally program in machine code.

3
01	LDA	50
02	ADC	51
03	STA	55
04	LDA	52
05	ADC	53
06	BPL	POS
07	LDA	55
08	PNT	
09	JMP	11
10	PNT	
11	END	

The contents of stores 50, 51, 52, 53 are 4, -3, 7, -8. Dry run this section of assembly language and determine the output. What would be the output if the contents of store 53 were changed to -5?

4   What are the similarities and differences between assembly language and machine code?

5   State two characteristics of high-level languages. Name four high-level languages and state their main areas of application.

6   State two factors which limit the portability of high-level languages.

7   State the purpose of utility and applications packages. Suggest three utility programs and three factors which could be used to assess the quality of an applications package.

8   State three examples of asplications packages.

9   (a)   (i) Give two short lines from a program in a high-level programming language you have learnt, each of which contains a different syntax error.
(ii) Give the correct versions of these lines.
(b)   State two types of software which can detect syntax errors.
(c)   State one way that a syntax error could be corrected on an interactive system.
(d)   Give two examples of run time errors in a program.
(e)   Give an example of an error which arises when using a program but which the computer cannot detect and say why the computer cannot detect it.
How would you detect such an error?

10   (a)   Explain why compilers and interpreters are needed.
(b)   Distinguish between syntax and execution errors, giving an example of each.
(c)   When developing a high-level language program using an interpreter it is possible that some syntax errors will not become apparent until the program is run. Explain why this is so and why it cannot occur if the program is being developed using a compiler.

(*d*) Compare the use of an interpreter and a compiler for:
(i) the development of high-level language programs;
(ii) the production of executable code for a developed program which is run frequently. (L)

OPERATING SYSTEMS

CONTENTS

The purpose of the operating system is to ensure that the computer system as a whole is used as **efficiently** as possible. It is fundamental to any use of the system and, therefore, loaded into the mainstore of the computer **as soon as the system is switched on**. In a microcomputer, and some minicomputers, it will be read from a **ROM chip**. In larger systems, requiring more complex operating systems, it will be loaded from **magnetic disc** using a **bootstrap routine**. Since the operating system itself is responsible for loading programs it is necessary to have a preliminary set of instructions, executed automatically, which will call the operating system from backing store – this is the bootstrap routine.

MAIN TASKS

Operating systems deal with mundane but essential **'background' processing details**. They **all**

1   allocate main store memory space to programs and load programs into that space;
2   transfer data and programs to and from backing store;
3   supervise the use of input and output devices;
4   provide the user interface, i.e. the software which allows the operator to communicate with the computer and possibly, in emergency, to interrupt execution of a program;
5   monitor the progress of the programs being run, providing error reports if necessary.

In more sophisticated systems which permit multiprogramming and multi-access (see p.112) the operating system also:

6   allocates job (program) priorities and sequencing to optimize CPU and peripheral usage;
7   determines the CPU allocation in a multi-access system and handles the memory and backing storage allocation to each terminal;
8   controls jobs without intervention from the operators, e.g. calling a compiler from disc when it is required. The data processing term 'job' describes a single unit of work; it includes the program, its data and its processing instructions.

One of the most common operating systems for microcomputers is **CP/M** – control program for microprocessors – but it is not standard. IBM, for instance, use PC-DOS (a version of MS-DOS) on their range of personal computers. This lack of standardization severely limits the **portability** of program software.

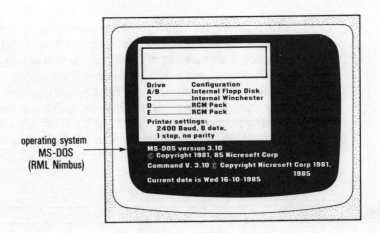

operating system
MS-DOS
(RML Nimbus)

```
Drive          Configuration
A/B ................Internal Flopp Disk
C ...................Internal Winchester
D ...................RCM Pack
E ...................RCM Pack
Printer settings:
    2400 Baud, 8 data,
    1 stop, no parity
MS-DOS version 3.10
ⓒ Copyright 1981, 85 Nicreseft Corp

Command V. 3.10 ⓒ Copyright Nicreseft Corp 1981,
                                              1985
Current date is Wed 16-10-1985
```

Figure 7.1 Screen monitor

Mainframe and, particularly, minicomputers are rather more standardized. Many use the powerful **UNIX** operating system which will support both multiprogramming and multi-access. Software run on UNIX need not be specially written for each machine, though some limited modifications may be required.

TYPES OF COMPUTER OPERATION

BATCH PROCESSING

In batch processing, jobs which share a **common language** are batched (grouped) together for processing. The rapidly falling cost of computers and the increasing power of smaller systems has reduced the importance of this mode of processing, which reached the pinnacle of its popularity when data preparation on punched cards was almost universal and the programs were executed on large mainframe systems at universities and computer bureaux.

In order to make the most efficient use of the processor, input cards were normally read to magnetic disc which then transferred the programs and data to the CPU at significantly higher speeds. Similarly, output from the CPU was **spooled** to magnetic disc for **off-line printing**.

During the early adoption of computers in schools and colleges programs were often prepared on punched cards, verified and taken to the local university for execution. There they would be processed as a batch.

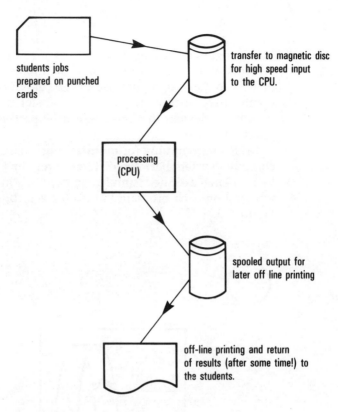

students jobs prepared on punched cards

transfer to magnetic disc for high speed input to the CPU.

processing (CPU)

spooled output for later off line printing

off-line printing and return of results (after some time!) to the students.

Figure 7.2 Batch processing

The example in Figure 7.2 characterizes the disadvantages of batch processing:

1 There is a **considerable time delay** from the completion of the program to its processing and return.
2 **No immediate action can be taken** to correct even the smallest of crash-inducing errors or to modify computer output.
   But:
3 Batch processing is **less expensive** than other operating systems.
4 The programmer does not need to be present during execution; this means that **the processing can be done at any time** convenient to the computer operator/computer bureau – possibly during the night.

Note: The student may find it confusing that 'batch processing' describes both an operating system and a method of data processing. The description of periodical payroll systems, billing systems and batch stock control systems as batch processes refers to the fact that **data** for these applications is handled as a batch.

Remote Job Entry (RJE) is a form of batch processing in which the user's job is transmitted to the computer from a remote peripheral, e.g. punched card reader.

MULTIPROGRAMMING AND MULTI-ACCESS

Multiprogramming and multi-access are integral to the operating systems of all modern mini- and mainframe computers. Their purpose is to make optimum use of the central processing unit, which operates so much **faster** than the transfer or operation rate of the peripheral devices that its time can be **partitioned** to different programs or users.

Multiprogramming (or **multitasking**) shares the CPU time of one computer system between **different programs**. The programs appear to be being executed simultaneously, but in fact the processor is working on each program in turn for very brief bursts of time. (See Figure 7.3.)

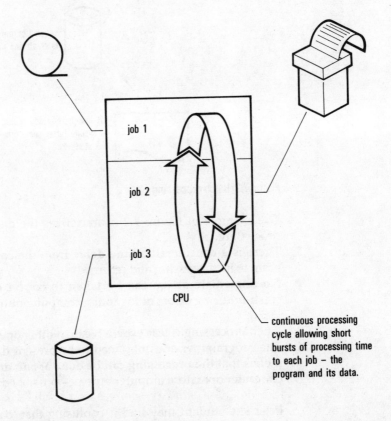

Figure 7.3 Multiprogramming

Multi-access (**time-sharing** or **multi-user**) systems share the CPU time between a **number of different terminals**, but the processing power of the CPU may provide each user with the illusion that he alone is using the system.

A **terminal** is any device from which data may be input to and/or output from the computer, e.g. teletypes, VDU workstations. The terminals may be physically connected to the CPU or linked via the telecommunications network using modems (see p.121). (See Figure 7.4.)

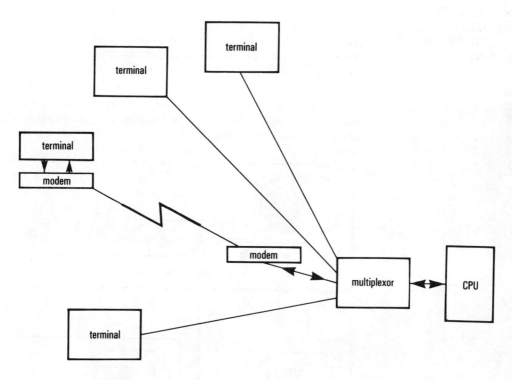

Figure 7.4 Multi-access system

INTERACTIVE PROCESSING

Multi-access systems provide interactive processing for multiple users. This mode of computer operation enables a **'conversation'** to take place between the user and the computer, as for example the question and answer process of interrogating a database.

The majority of **microcomputers** will only permit interactive use – a single user running one program at a time.

Other examples of multi-access interactive applications are:

1 **Bank cashpoint tills**;
2 **Large database enquiry services**, e.g. British Rail travel enquiries and, increasingly, telephone directory services using 'keyword' searches.
3 **Reservation systems.**

Do not be confused here. **Multiprogramming** shares the time of the CPU between a **number of programs**, while **multi-access** shares the CPU time between **a number of users**.

Many of the operating systems for mainframe and minicomputers, e.g. Unix, will support **both** multiprogramming and multi-access. They will also assign program or terminal **priorities** to concentrate processing time on the most urgent tasks.

LOCAL AREA NETWORKS (LANs)

LANs are built around the computer system of a relatively small geographical area such as a university campus, a school or, most frequently, a single building. The computers may be distributed in several rooms or concentrated in one. Most users – while having a

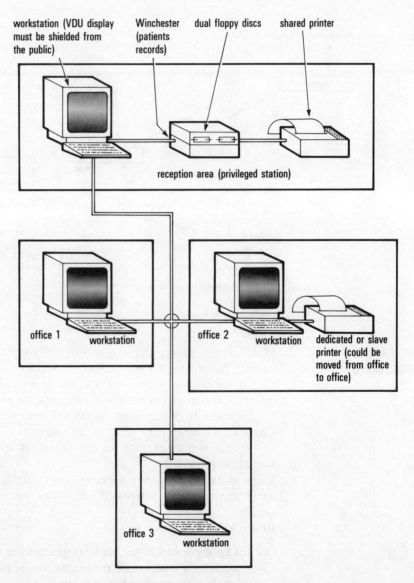

workstation (VDU display must be shielded from the public)   Winchester (patients records)   dual floppy discs   shared printer

reception area (privileged station)

office 1   workstation

office 2   workstation   dedicated or slave printer (could be moved from office to office)

office 3   workstation

Figure 7.5 Local area network in a medical practice

constant need for the computer, keyboard and monitor – will require **peripheral units** such as a printer or a graph plotter **much less frequently**. LANs enable all the devices in a network to communicate with each other and the users will have access to its shared resources: fixed discs (which could store commonly required files), floppy discs, printers and plotters. These units are then used much more frequently and are therefore more cost effective.

Some LANs contain at least one central or privileged station from which the system as a whole can be controlled – the system manager's station. It could, for instance, be used to send a message to all the workstations simultaneously, or to disenable a particular station.

In Case Study 1, the final configuration of the system is an example of a local area network established around a central minicomputer. Another example, illustrated opposite, is the use of a LAN in a medical practice. Each of the doctors will have a workstation in his office and all will have access to the patients' records.

The three most common LAN configurations are shown in Figure 7.6. Some configurations, like the Cambridge Ring, define a central controlling computer through which instructions are guided to the correct device. In others, like the Ethernet, each device listens continuously and identifies its own address when this is transmitted. In all LAN configurations, the devices are **physically connected** using special cabling. Networks covering larger geographical areas (**wide area networks, WANs**) such as PRESTEL, where cabling would be impractical, use the telecommunications network to permit multiple users access to a number of remote mini- and mainframe databases.

The continuing changeover of the telecommunications network from an **analogue to a digital** base (see chapter 8) is expected to make **networking** (which could then be installed as an extension to the company's PABX system) and **communications** the next big growth area in the computer field.

All network users are required to **log on** to the system. Each user has a **personal password** which identifies him to the system and provides access to his **private files**. In some systems which support **electronic mail** (see p.127) the password will also enable the user to determine if any messages have been left since he last used the system.

Networks with more than one processor are described as **distributed processing systems**. The operating system of these networks can determine how best to distribute the processing load, whether it will be done by the principal computer or others with which it will communicate.

REAL-TIME PROCESSING

In real-time processing, making it distinct from interactive computing, it is the response **in real time** which is **vital**. No attempt is made to distribute the power of the processor – its attention is concentrated solely on a single task. Real-time systems process and

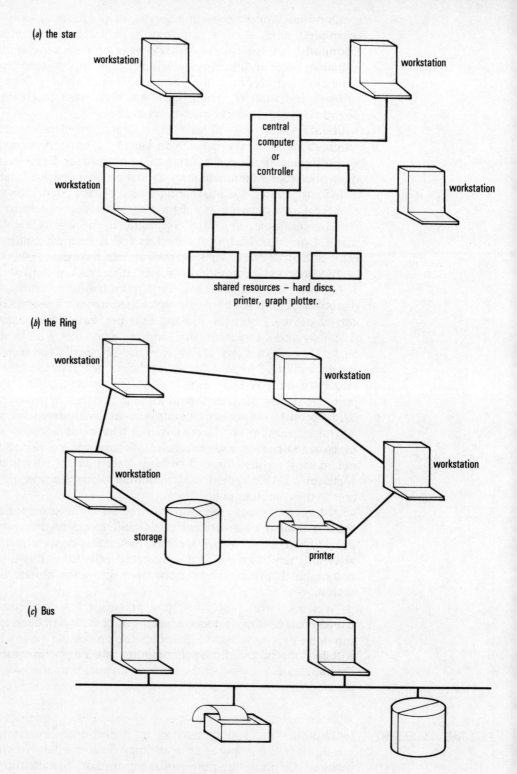

(a) the star

workstation

workstation

central
computer
or
controller

workstation

workstation

shared resources – hard discs,
printer, graph plotter.

(b) the Ring

workstation

workstation

workstation

workstation

storage

printer

(c) Bus

Figure 7.6 Local area network configurations

respond to data rapidly enough to influence its source. Typical examples are:

1 Monitoring the control of a chemical reaction to ensure that important variables such as temperature remain within defined limits.
2 Directional control of vehicles in space.
3 Automatic railway signalling.
4 Control of missiles in flight.
5 Nuclear reactor control.
6 Sophisticated pilot training simulators.

Both **real-time** and **interactive** processing are **on-line**, i.e. there is a direct link to the CPU. Batch processing, as we have seen, is normally **off-line**.

SUMMARY:	
1	The operating system is fundamental to any computer system; it deals with the mundane but essential 'background' processing details such as transferring programs/data to and from backing store and providing the user interface.
2	The operating system is loaded into the computer as soon as it is switched on and runs continuously while it remains on. It is either read from a ROM chip or loaded from magnetic disc using a bootstrap routine.
3	A 'job' describes a single processing task: the program, its data and the operating instructions.
4	Batch processing systems group together jobs which share a common language.
5	Multiprogramming shares the time of the CPU between a number of different programs.
6	Multi-access shares the time of the CPU between a number of different users.
7	Interactive processing describes a 'conversational' mode of computer operation in which one or more users are linked directly with the CPU, e.g. bank cashpoint systems.
8	In real-time processing, the response in real time is vital; such systems process data and respond so rapidly that they are able to influence the source of the data, e.g. control applications.
9	Interactive and real-time processes are on-line. Batch processing is normally off-line.
10	A local area network (LAN) allows a group of users in a limited geographical area to share the resources of a system. All the devices in the system are physically connected together with special cabling, allowing any device to communicate with any other device.
11	All network users are required to log on to the network using a password which personally identifies them to the system.
12	Networks with more than one processor are described as distributed processing systems.

1 State three tasks of an operating system. Name one operating system commonly found on microcomputers and a second on mini- or main-frame computers.

2 State whether each of the applications shown below is (i) batch; (ii) on-line; (iii) computer control.
   (a) Chemical manufacturing process
   (b) Company payroll
   (c) Computerized theatre seat booking
   (d) Industrial robot   (M)

3 State one advantage and one disadvantage of batch processing.

4 (a) What is meant by a multi-access computers?
   (b) Why do users of multi-access computers usually have to have a user's password?
   (c) Three levels of access to files held on a computer backing store are: read and write; read only; forbidden.
      Give an appropriate situation for each of these.
   (d) Give three actions that must be taken by the operating system of a multi-access computer to organize the work of everyone using it.

5 Describe the distinction between multi-access and multi-programming.

6 State one advantage and one disadvantage of local area networks.

7 How does on-line computing differ from real-time computing?

8 (a) Explain what real-time processing is.
   (b) Describe an application where a computer system is needed for real-time process control.
   (c) For this application of real-time process control, describe
      (i) the data which is needed by the computer;
      (ii) how the data is captured, including how it is validated;
      (iii) the processing that is done;
      (iv) output signals from the computer and how these signals produce the necessary effects.   (L)

DATA COMMUNICATIONS – THE CONVERGING TECHNOLOGIES

CONTENTS

MODEMS

We have already seen that modems and the telecommunications network (including microwave and satellite links) can be used to connect a terminal **on-line** to a remote computer.

The same technique can be used to link any devices, provided the correct **protocols** (data formats) are used or the **handshake** routines (signal exchanges to establish communication) are confirmed. Telephone lines, for instance, have been used commercially for many years for **telex** and **facsimile** transmissions. Telex forms a link between two teleprinters so that what is keyed on the transmitting machine will also appear on the (remote) receiving machine. Facsimile is similar but it allows the transmission of complete pages, including graphics, by **digitizing** the document for transmission and decoding it at its destination.

Modems provide the interface between the **digital computer** and the **analogue telephone network**. Digital signals are MOdulated for transmission and DEModulated for input to the receiving device.

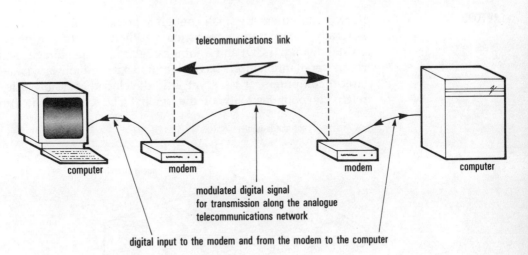

Figure 8.1 Modem communication link

Modern systems generally use modems which connect **directly** to the telephone network and, with appropriate software, establish the telephone connection automatically. These modems are **faster** and **more**

reliable than the earlier **acoustic couplers** which simply use the handset of an ordinary telephone.

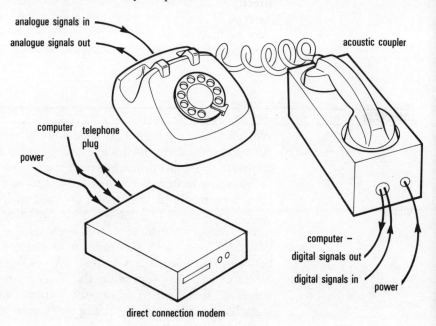

Figure 8.2　Direct connection modem and acoustic coupler

LAPTOPS

Laptop computers are small enough to be easily carried around. They normally incorporate a restricted width dot matrix printer, liquid crystal display (LCD) and a mini-cassette for data storage. Although computer manufacturers have identified a potentially large market for laptop computers, it is as yet little developed; possibly due to the relatively poor legibility of the small LCD screens. The future of

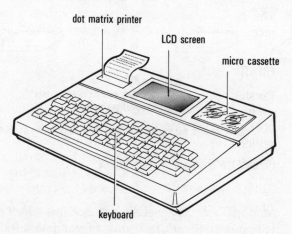

Figure 8.2A　Laptop computer

laptop sales is thought to lie with travelling businessmen and company representatives. Using a modem, laptops could **communicate directly** with the company's central computer. Orders placed with the reps could be transmitted daily, or even confirmed at the time of placement using the customer's telephone; the printer would then be used to provide a receipt or written confirmation of the transaction.

VIEWDATA AND TELETEXT

Viewdata and Teletext describe database systems which display information to the public using the television screen.

VIEWDATA

Viewdata permits two-way communication by connecting the users' microcomputer to the database computers using a modem, i.e. it is an **interactive** Teletext system. Alternatively, an ordinary television set could be used in conjunction with a viewdata terminal; control of the system is then achieved with a special keypad.

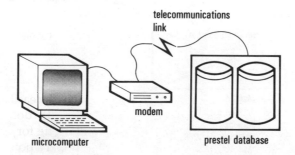

Figure 8.3 Connecting a microcomputer to the Prestel database system

The best example in this country is the **Prestel system** and, more recently, TTNS (The Times Network for Schools).

PRESTEL

Prestel users are identified to the system by their **password**; the system responds by greeting the user by name and the user is then able to interrogate the database. This is a **menu driven** process in which the user is presented with a successive series of menus, each of which narrows down the search for the information he requires. If, for example, we were to use the system to find the cost of a first-class rail ticket from Exeter to London, the system would provide the series of menus shown in Figure 8.4A.

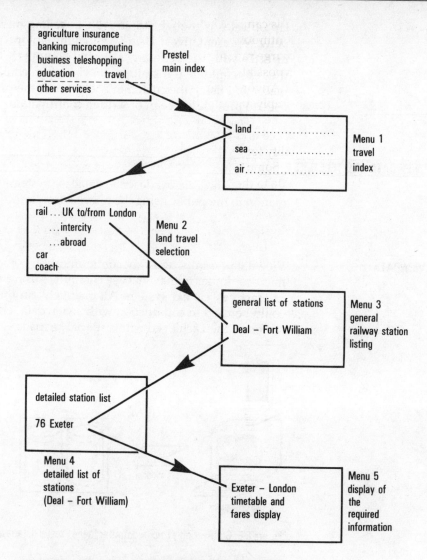

agriculture insurance
banking microcomputing
business teleshopping
education   travel
─────────────
other services

Prestel
main index

land ....
sea ....
air ....

Menu 1
travel
index

rail ... UK to/from London
       ...intercity
       ...abroad
car
coach

Menu 2
land travel
selection

general list of stations

Deal – Fort William

Menu 3
general
railway station
listing

detailed station list

76 Exeter

Menu 4
detailed list of
stations
(Deal – Fort William)

Exeter – London
timetable and
fares display

Menu 5
display of
the
required
information

Figure 8.4A Using Prestel

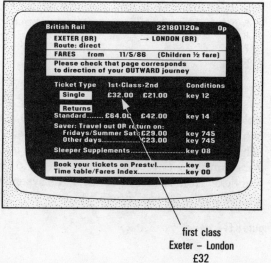

British Rail   221801120a   0p
EXETER (BR)   ⟶ LONDON (BR)
Route: direct
FARES   from   11/5/86   (Children ½ fare)
Please check that page corresponds
to direction of your OUTWARD journey

Ticket Type   1st·Class›2nd   Conditions
Single   £32.00   £21.00   key 12
Returns
Standard........£64.00   £42.00   key 14
Saver: Travel out OR return on:
  Fridays/Summer Sat £29.00   key 745
  Other days.............£23.00   key 745
Sleeper Supplements...............   key 08

Book your tickets on Prestel...............key 8
Time table/Fares Index...................key 00

Figure 8.4B Fares display

first class
Exeter – London
£32

This can be a lengthy and expensive process – the telephone line is in continuous use even though most connections are made at local charge rate. If the user knows the page number which he requires, it is possible to move to that page **directly**.

Anyone can become an **information provider** to Prestel – they simply pay for the number of pages which they require – though some would-be political users of the system have not been allocated space and questions have also been raised about the legal responsibility for the database content.

Some other Prestel facilities are listed below; some are only available to the subscribers of **closed user groups** (see question 4).

Gateways The biggest user of the system is the **travel business**. Gateways permit travel agents to access the holiday company computers and to confirm bookings or make detailed enquiries. It is estimated that 80 per cent of Thompson and Horizon holidays are booked using the Viewdata system. The system is very user friendly and presents less of a training problem than the use of traditional timetables and brochures.

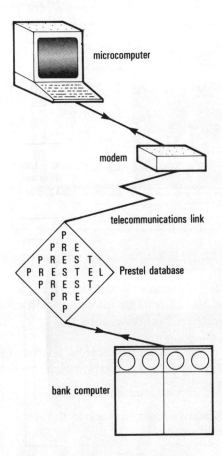

Figure 8.5A Prestel – Bank of Scotland

Home banking These services use a similar structure, allowing the user to access his bank or building society accounts at any time which he finds convenient.

Figure 8.5B   Bank of Scotland title page

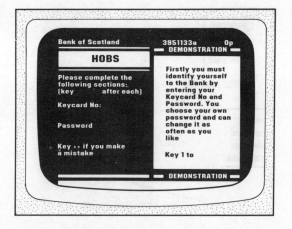

Figure 8.5C   Bank of Scotland demo page, showing the password checks

Home shopping is a similar system which allows the user to select goods and either pay directly by quoting a cash card number, or have the amount added to his Prestel account.

Chat facility for the hard of hearing has been particularly successful. Both parties holding the 'conversation' need to be on line to Prestel simultaneously.

Micronet 800 allows users who access the system using microcomputers to download software.

ELECTRONIC MAIL

Subscribers to **Telecom Gold** and other electronic mail systems are able to leave messages for one another using the **mailbox facility**. Messages can be left or accessed at any time; the system will notify the user of a waiting message when he next accesses it. Obviously, to be successful, all the members of a group who would normally need to communicate must be Telecom Gold members and must also access the system regularly; anyone leaving a message needs to feel confident that it will be received.

The increased installation of **local area networks (LANs)** and their future potential will extend the use of electronic mail for inter-office communication, and the **speed** of transmission will be of great benefit to companies with widely dispersed units. Its future is closely linked with the rapid adoption of **word processing systems** (see next section) and, although electronic mail is currently limited to text messages, their combination may ultimately be the foundation of many **electronic or paperless offices**.

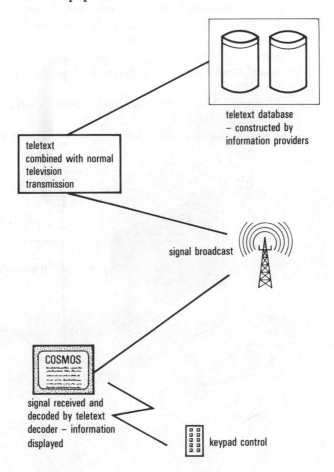

Figure 8.6 Teletext transmission

TELETEXT

Teletext systems, such as **CeeFax** and **Oracle**, provide only one-way communication. Information is transmitted along with the normal television signal using 'spare' lines not required for the television picture. Television sets with teletext decoders can capture these lines to construct pages of information.

Information providers are able to give the public 'up-to-the-minute' information such as train cancellations, flight delays, the latest weather forecast. Pages are selected from successive menus in a similar way to Prestel, but one drawback of Teletext is the length of time taken to reach a selected page – **cycle time**, which effectively limits the number of pages available to the system. One application of the system is to provide **subtitles** to television programmes for the hard of hearing.

WORD PROCESSING

Word processors may be **dedicated systems** – designed solely for word processing – or **software enhancements** to general-purpose systems. Dedicated systems will be preferable for ease of operation, but all word processing systems include:

1   **a keyboard** – possibly with special function keys;
2   **the CPU**;
3   **Magnetic disc backing storage** – either dual floppy discs or a Winchester hard disc;
4   **a screen monitor** – high resolution and flicker-free;

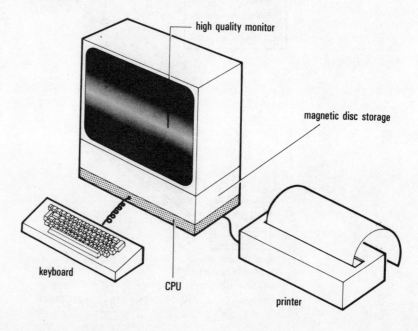

Figure 8.7 A wordprocessing system

5   **a printer** – word processors are intended for correspondence, so a daisywheel printer would be ideal. Other possibilities are an ink-jet printer which is virtually silent in operation, or a dot-matrix printer with NLQ (near letter quality) option which provides the flexibility of higher speed draft quality output.

Word processors will:

1   allow the keyed text to be **edited**. This will include not only simple error correction but also the **deletion**, **repositioning** and **duplication** of complete sections of text, e.g. the movement of a paragraph to a different position.

2   **store and retrieve text** from backing storage. Text storage allows the basic outline of a frequently used letter to be retained (details such as name are edited in at the time of use) or complete documents to be formed from **standard paragraphs**. This process is now commonly used to create individual contracts of employment and is certainly used by Midshire in Case Study 1.

Figure 8.8 Personalizing a basic letter using a wordprocessing system

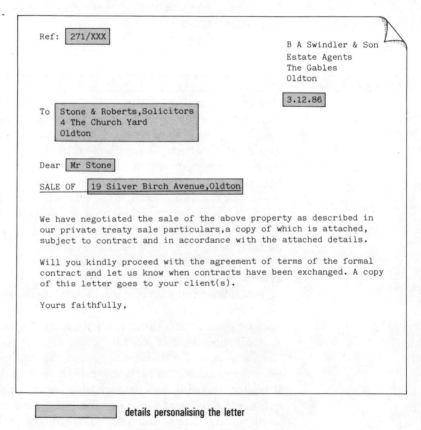

Ref: 271/XXX

                                          B A Swindler & Son
                                          Estate Agents
                                          The Gables
                                          Oldton

                                          3.12.86

To   Stone & Roberts,Solicitors
     4 The Church Yard
     Oldton

Dear Mr Stone

SALE OF   19 Silver Birch Avenue,Oldton

We have negotiated the sale of the above property as described in
our private treaty sale particulars,a copy of which is attached,
subject to contract and in accordance with the attached details.

Will you kindly proceed with the agreement of terms of the formal
contract and let us know when contracts have been exchanged. A copy
of this letter goes to your client(s).

Yours faithfully,

☐   details personalising the letter

Will you kindly   standard format – stored text

Some systems enable a basic letter outline to be used in conjunction with a file which contains the names and addresses of the intended recipients. The same letter can then be **personalized** automatically and sent to a number of different people; for example, an estate agent may wish to inform several potential purchasers of a new property which he has been commissioned to sell.

Other useful features are **justification** for creating straight edges to the text of a letter; **search and replace** for changing a name or correcting a word spelt wrongly throughout the text, and **line wrap** which automatically places words which are too long for one line on the next.

Despite the advantages of word processors and the potential of electronic mail, which is already used widely in the United States, the difficulties of their introduction should not be underestimated:

1 **Staff co-operation is essential** – new skills need to be learned and new system 'teething difficulties' may arise.
2 **Staff will need to be trained** if they are to handle the new equipment (e.g. word processors) with confidence.
3 **The initial cost** of the equipment may be substantial.
4 Care will need to be given to **the siting of VDU workstations** in order to minimize the potential negative effects on health such as eye-strain and general fatigue.

CONVERGING TECHNOLOGIES

One of the most far-reaching changes in communications technology has already begun. The telephone network, some parts of which were designed over 100 years ago, is being transformed from an **analogue to a digital system**. This will mean that all transmissions along the telephone network will be **digitally coded**; computers and their major communication system will then both handle information represented in the same form. One effect will be that modems will no longer be required; another, that all conversations will be **digitally encoded**. This **analogue to digital conversion** will require speech to be sampled 8000 times a second in order that it can be reconstructed exactly. The routing and switching will also be provided by a digital system.

While the problems of digital encoding of speech for transmission differ from those of voice recognition systems, the progress in that area may well focus greater attention on the use of voice recognition systems for computer control.

In addition, the traditional copper cabling used for telephone systems is unsuitable for high-speed high-density data communications. It is already being replaced by **fibre optics cable**, which consists of extremely fine strands of flexible, incredibly pure glass. The communications data – **transmitted as pulses of light** – will be little affected by interference (noise), while signal regenerators – capable of restoring the original signal – will be much more widely spaced than the copper cabling analogue repeaters which necessarily amplified the interference along with the signal.

The merging of computer and communications technologies is often called information technology.

PACKET SWITCHING SERVICE

The packet switching service is employed commercially to link computer systems. It provides a **fast**, **cheap** and **virtually error-free** method of data transmission. The text is divided into a series of packets, each sharing a common structure and labelled with its destination. The packets are then channelled from computer to computer and reassembled for processing at their final destination.

INTEGRATED SERVICES DIGITAL NETWORK (ISDN)

The next significant step will be the integration of all the present communications services – telex, speech facsimile, packet switching service and others – into a single line known as the ISDN line. Instead of the special cabling and connections required for some services at the moment, business subscribers would have complete freedom of choice from a single multi-service workstation made feasible by their compatibility.

SUMMARY:

1 Modems provide the interface between digital computers and the analogue telephone system; they will not be required when the transformation of the telephone system to digital operation is complete.

2 Viewdata and Teletext systems display information to the public using the television screen.

3 Viewdata provides two-way communication with the database – the best example in this country is Prestel.

4 Prestel facilitates services in addition to database enquiries. These include home banking, home shopping, gateways to other computers and electronic mail. Some of these are available only to the subscribers of closed user groups.

5 Teletext systems such as CeeFax and Oracle provide only one-way communication. The information is transmitted using the spare lines of normal television transmission.

6 Word processors are having a significant impact on office practice. They consist of a keyboard, monitor, disc storage, CPU and a printer; they manipulate, store and edit text. The final printed copy is always perfect.

7 Electronic mail and word processors could form the basis of the electronic office of the future. Some difficulties related to their introduction include the need for staff training, staff co-operation and the initial cost.

8 The telephone network is being transformed from an analogue to a digital system. This means that computers and their communication system will, for the first time, handle information represented in the same form.

9 Fibre optics cabling is replacing traditional cabling in the telephone network. It consists of extremely fine strands of flexible, incredibly pure glass.

10 The packet switching service (PSS) provides a fast, cheap, virtually error-free method of data transmission between computers.

11 The next significant step for communications services will be the complete integration of all the present services: the integrated services digital network (ISDN).

CHAPTER 8 QUESTIONS

1 Why are two modems required to complete a communications link? State one example of the use of a modem-based communications link.

2 There are two basic types of Teletext services. distinguish between them, illustrating your answer with examples of the two services.

3 The diagram below shows two different ways of using a television set to display information transmitted from a distant computer.

(a) Which of Ceefax, Oracle and Prestel is an example of service 2?

(b) In service 2, special devices labelled X in the diagram are needed at each end of the telephone line. What are these devices called and why are they needed?

(c) Service 2 can be used to carry out different tasks from service 1. Give two examples of these tasks.

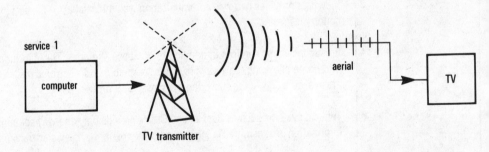

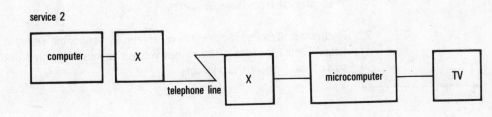

(*d*)   Give two reasons why service 2 can provide facilities that service 1 cannot.

4   What is a 'closed user group'?

5   Describe four uses of the Prestel system.

6   Give two advantages of the electronic mail system and one disadvantage.

7   To send a letter with an electronic mail system, you would type it in on your keyboard and it would be sent to the central computer. Each time that you connect to the computer you will be given a list of the letters waiting for you.

(*a*)   Given one advantage of electronic mail compared with sending a letter by post.

(*b*)   Given one advantage compared with using a telephone.

(*c*)   Post Office workers are concerned over the widespread use of electronic mail. Give one reason for this concern.

(*d*)   Give an example of an item which could not be sent by electronic mail.   (L)

8   Choose a job which will be improved or made easier by the increased use of electronic mail and explain why.   (N – part only)

9   Describe a situation which would be appropriate for the installation of a LAN. State two general characteristics of such situations.

10   State four essential features of a word processing system; two advantages of a word processing system over traditional typewriters and one disadvantage.

11   Give a brief description of:
(*a*)   the Packet Switching Service;
(*b*)   the Integrated Services Digital Network.

COMPUTER PERSONNEL

CONTENTS

The detailed job specification of personnel with data processing responsibility will vary from company to company. The individual tasks described below are those typically defined in the operation of a **large** mainframe computer system. If the central company computer is smaller – a minicomputer – some tasks such as computer operator may not be required; the number of personnel will be reduced and some of the separate tasks will be amalgamated into single job specifications. Candidates should place their emphasis **on understanding the task descriptions rather than learning job titles or management structures.**

The diagram below shows the overall personnel structure. Note that the majority of the tasks involve using, maintaining or enhancing the existing system (solid). The responsibility of a smaller number of staff lies in the development and implementation of new systems (dotted).

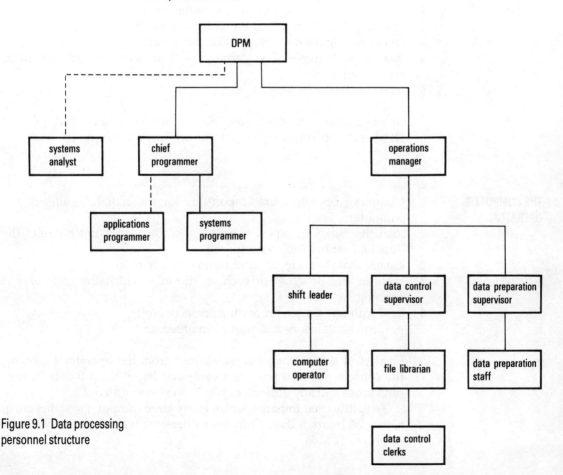

Figure 9.1 Data processing personnel structure

PERSONNEL STRUCTURE

THE DATA PROCESSING MANAGER

The DPM has overall responsibility for the data processing department. In large companies this will be an administrative appointment which includes:

1   overall financial responsibility for the department;
2   the final decision on new projects which the department will undertake;
3   the appointment of new departmental staff and the career progress of those already within the department;
4   the allocation of specific tasks to his section managers;
5   the recommendation (and justification) of system improvements and, more generally, advising the company on possible applications of newly available technology.

THE OPERATIONS MANAGER

The operations manager will have substantial practical experience of computer operations and be responsible for the day-to-day management. This responsibility will include:

1   ensuring that the computer is adequately maintained.
2   ensuring that the required stationery is available.
3   co-ordinating the data preparation and control.
4   dealing with day-to-day staffing problems such as shift rotations, staff absences.
5   liaison with the DPM.

In a small computer operation, this post will be combined with that of DPM as it is in Midshire District Council (see Case Study 1).

THE COMPUTER OPERATOR

Computer operators are responsible for the actual running of the computers. They will:

1   load the magnetic tapes, magnetic discs or (much more rarely) the punched cards which are required;
2   ensure that the correct output stationery is in place;
3   monitor the progress of each of the jobs which the computer is running;
4   deal with any simple processing errors or faults;
5   perform straightforward, routine maintenance.

Control of the computer is maintained from the **operator's console**; the console will also provide a **computer log** of the job details, running times and any difficulties which were encountered.

To justify their initial expense, many large computer systems are in action 24 hours a day. Computer operators will therefore normally work in shifts. The first promotion will be to chief operator, then to shift leader.

DATA PREPARATION STAFF

We have already noted that the most common method of data capture is still written forms. The data preparation staff convert the original information into data suitable for input to the computer.

Traditionally this required transcription to punched cards or paper tape, but the most common method today is **direct data entry using key-to-disc or key-to-tape**.

In some promotional structures the next step for data preparation staff is data control.

DATA CONTROL STAFF

The data control staff ensure that the data for each job, possibly from different departments, is assembled for the processing run. They are also responsible for returning the processed data to the user as quickly as possible and, if necessary, allocating job priorities.

Large departments may have a separate **file librarian** whose task involves:

1 storing the computer tapes and discs.
2 keeping a record of their use.
3 ensuring their good physical condition; and
4 preventing unauthorized access.

THE SYSTEMS ANALYST

The systems analyst is responsible for analysing current working methods or specific proposals in order to determine their suitability for computerization; for recommending a detailed computer system and controlling its introduction.

The first stage will be to carry out a **feasibility study** on the existing system or proposal. This may involve:

1 interviewing the present management and staff.
2 looking in detail at the work being done and the methods which are used.
3 defining the main stages: its source of information, the process which is required and the purpose and form of the end product.

In his report the systems analyst will describe the existing system and present an alternative (or improved) computer system. His recommendations will take particular account of:

1 the initial and running costs of the new system in relation to the old; and
2 the costs or difficulties which may arise in the introduction of a suitable method of data capture and/or transcription.

The report will normally contain a **systems flowchart** which describes the new system and shows how its parts are related. For this purpose the standard systems flowchart symbols shown below are used.

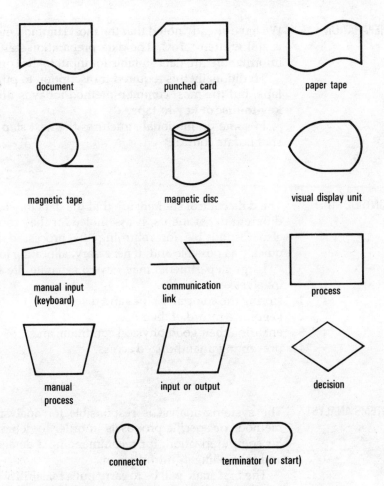

Figure 9.2 Program and systems flowchart symbols

If his recommendations are accepted, the systems analyst will then be responsible for their implementation:

1 He will provide detailed methods of data capture, processing and output.

2 The necessary software will be written by an **applications programmer** (after consultation with the chief programmer), but the systems analyst may well be involved in the production of suitable test data which will ensure that the programs are thoroughly tested for all permutations of data entry.

3 He may advise his clients on the need for **staff training** and preparation.

4 During the actual implementation, the manual and computer systems will run **in parallel** for a time. During this phase the systems analyst

will check that the personnel thoroughly understand their tasks and that any unforeseen problems are corrected.

Example:

A large mail order company decides to open shops in some cities on a trial basis to sell directly to the public. The management decides that the public will make their selections from catalogues in the shops and that the sale will take place in two parts:

1 The POS assistant will use the item code, presented by the customer, to determine the availability of the item in stock.
2 If availability and the customer's intent to purchase are confirmed, the sale will proceed.

The company wish to introduce a multi-access system for sales and stock control. Show how their requirements will be presented in a systems flowchart drawn up by the systems analyst.

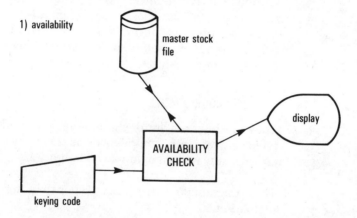

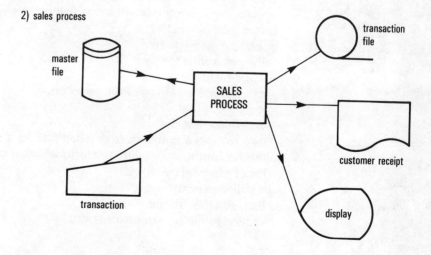

Figure 9.3 Sales and stock control

PROGRAMMERS

Large departments will distinguish between two categories of programmer:

APPLICATIONS PROGRAMMERS

They write the programs for new systems applications, such as those determined by the systems analyst. These programs are normally written in **high-level language** and in large applications a group of programmers, each writing a **program module**, may be involved.

A significant proportion of applications software is now written by specialist software houses, e.g. Logica, either on a commissioned basis or in response to their own market research.

In addition many successful applications packages have already been written by vocational specialists, e.g. a civil engineering package written by a civil engineer. Some writers, noting the ease with which new high-level languages and computer systems can be programmed, predict that the number of applications programmers will fall. The programs will then be written either by the user himself or by the systems analyst.

SYSTEMS PROGRAMMERS

They are responsible for the maintenance and development of systems software, e.g. compilers or operating systems. These programs are normally written in **low-level language**.

The programmers are also responsible for the program **documentation**.

User documentation

This provides users with detailed instructions on how to load and operate the program; it will avoid detailed technical or programming comments, but includes:
1 operating instructions
2 the input format for data
3 output details or options
4 any relevant limitations of the program.

Technical documentation

This provides a much more detailed insight into the program and is aimed at computer operators or technicians. It will include:
1 a list of program variables
2 a detailed program flowchart
3 a listing of the program
4 technical limitations of the program.

Handwritten margin notes:

when a fixed number of bits is available to store a long binary number like this, it must be TRUNCATED or cut to fit.

eg
if 4 bits are available to store a representation of 0·8, we can truncate the recurring binary no + store 0·8 as

$\frac{1}{2}$ s $\frac{1}{4}$ s $\frac{1}{8}$ s $\frac{1}{16}$ s

1   1   0   0

this binary no is = to 0·75 so we have introduced a truncation error of 0·05 by attempting to store 0·8 in 4 bits.

better approximation if we round the binary fraction

if bit = 1 we round up
if 0 we round down

The decimal 0·8 can be stored in 4 bits as 0·1101

$\frac{1}{2}$ s $\frac{1}{4}$ s $\frac{1}{8}$ s $\frac{1}{16}$ s

1   1   0   1

= binary no = 0·8125

we have rounding error of 0·0125.

All the posts described above are examples of jobs created by the computer industry. The impact of computers on general employment is discussed in chapter 12.

SUMMARY:

1 Job titles and management structures will vary from company to company. Candidates should place more emphasis on the task definition than on its title.

2 The DPM has overall responsibility for the data processing department.

3 The operations manager has day-to-day responsibility.

4 Systems analysts are responsible for determining the potential of processes or proposals for computerization. Their recommendation will be made after a feasibility study. If the report is accepted, systems analysts are then responsible for the implementation of their recommendations.

5 A systems analyst will often use a systems flowchart to describe a computer system.

6 Applications programmers write applications packages. They may work within a data processing department on tasks defined by the systems analyst; in a specialist software house on commissioned tasks or those identified by in-house research; or have vocational experience of the task. Applications programmers generally write in high-level languages.

7 Systems programmers are responsible for maintaining and developing systems software, e.g. a compiler. They will write extensively in machine code.

8 Computer programmers are also responsible for the computer documentation. This includes both user and technical documentation.

9 Other tasks includes computer operation, data preparation and data control.

10 All the defined tasks are examples of jobs created by the computer industry.

CHAPTER 9 QUESTIONS

1 Describe the responsibilities of the DPM in a large data processing department.

2 Describe the promotional ladder which might be available to a capable youngster, with good grades at GCSE, initially appointed as a trainee programmer in a large computer department.

3 In what major way has the task of a data processing clerk changed over the last fifteen years?

4 Describe four tasks of a computer operator.

5 A large data processing department may have a chief programmer. What additional responsibilities (to those of a programmer) would you expect within his post specification?

6   What kind of qualifications and experience would you expect from an applicant for the post of systems analyst? Are there any personal attributes of particular importance? Why?

7   A company decides to use a computer to keep its accounts.

   The company could (i) use a computer bureau to process the data or (ii) could use in-house processing facilities.

   Give one advantage of each method.   (L)

8   State three tasks performed by the systems analyst.

9   A firm which has not yet used a computer has ordered one for delivery in a year's time. State three things which the firm should do to prepare for the arrival of the computer.   (L)

10   Some large processing departments have programmers with separate responsiblilities. What are their tasks?

11   State three items to be found in the user documentation and three to be found in the technical documentation.

THE CASE STUDY APPROACH

CONTENTS

INTRODUCTION

With only one exception, the examining groups have incorporated case studies into the structure of their GCSE computer studies examination; but within this generalization lies considerable variation.

The case studies are based on existing or potential computer applications and are presented to the candidate either:

1   as a detailed description of the application prepared by the examining group.
2   by adopting an existing, commercially available package, *or*
3   as a broad definition of the application by the examining group.

The way in which the case study is examined also varies. In some cases a complete paper is devoted to the case study; alternatively, case study questions can be integrated into papers with general examining objectives.

In the majority of cases, the case study for a particular year is clearly stated in the syllabus and either its commercial source or its description is available at the commencement of the course. However, at the time of writing one group (London and East Anglia) do not provide the case study until the first paper is taken; it is then examined in paper 2.

It is essential that you ensure:

(*a*)   that you know the case study for your examination as early as possible;
(*b*)   that if it is defined within the syllabus you obtain either the details provided by the examining group or the commercial package which the examining group has nominated;
(*c*)   that you are aware how it will be examined – whether there will be a separate paper or whether the case study questions will be integrated into general papers.

Case studies draw particular attention to three facets of computing:

1   The flow of data through a computer system
2   The encoding of data for a computer application
3   The appreciation of the level of computing power which is necessary for a particular application; also an informed opinion on the most appropriate peripherals for a particular application, given the user specification.

The case studies in this chapter have been chosen to emphasize the possible variety of such studies and to facilitate structuring a broad range of typical 'case study' questions. Both of the studies are heavily based on existing real-life applications.

Case Study 1 describes the early adoption of a computing system by a county council, its use of the system and the progressive upgrading.

Case Study 2 describes the use of a microcomputer in a typical small business application.

THE DISTRICT COUNCIL

John North was appointed Data Processing Manager (DPM) for Midshire District Council in 1980. In common with many local authorities, Midshire had been swift to recognize the potential of computers. As early as 1974, the Council had introduced a computer system to:

(i) improve the efficiency of the production of rate demand notices and the collection of rates;

(ii) handle the staff payroll.

Both of these applications were ideal for computerization.

(i) RATES

All properties have a rateable value determined by the District Council; this is a largely unchanging figure. Each year the District Council prepares a budget and from this determines a rate per pound of rateable value which it will set in order to meet the budget requirements. The rate demand for each household or business can then be determined by multiplying the rateable value by the rate in the pound. This is a **standard** and **repetitive** process.

The Midshire District Council computerized rating system covered two major aspects:

1 the preparation and distribution of rate demands;
2 the payment of those demands.

The initial system incorporated a **line printer** for output and relied on punched cards for **data storage**, **input** and **alternative output**. Each ratepayer had up to five cards:

two for the **standing details** (name, address, parish reference number, rating class);

one for the **rate demand**;

one for **credits** to his account; and

one for any **variations** such as change of ownership or usage.

The first two cards were punched and verified by data preparation clerks from information supplied, on written forms, by householders and businesses throughout the District. The third card was produced automatically as output from the computer system:

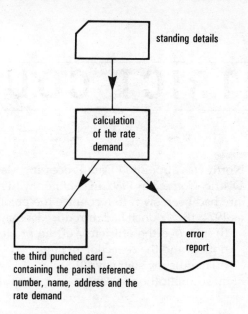

Figure 10.1 Rate calculation

This card was then used to print the rate demand notices **off-line**.

Payments to the District Council could either be made by post or by calling personally at the Council offices. In either case the payment made was encoded on the fourth card. The third and fourth cards could then be compared so as to determine any outstanding debts.

(ii) STAFF PAYROLL

Company payrolls were among the first computer applications. Again, it is a repetitive task in which the employee's net pay is calculated from his gross pay using **standard** rules.

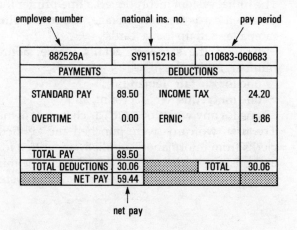

Figure 10.1A A typical computerized payslip

Figure 10.2 The initial
payroll system

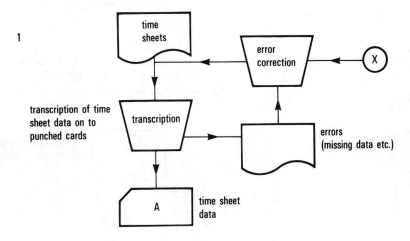

1

time
sheets

error
correction

X

transcription of time
sheet data on to
punched cards

transcription

errors
(missing data etc.)

A

time sheet
data

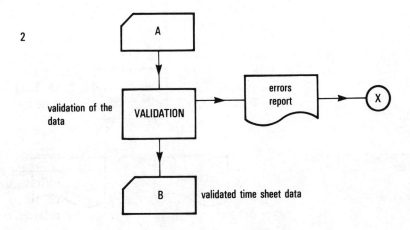

2

A

validation of the
data

VALIDATION

errors
report

X

B

validated time sheet data

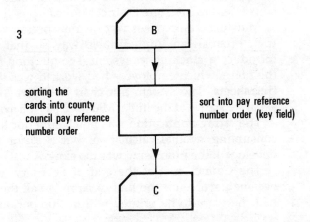

3

B

sorting the
cards into county
council pay reference
number order

sort into pay reference
number order (key field)

C

Figure 10.2B

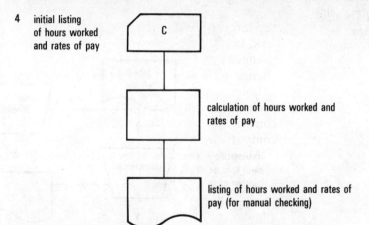

4   initial listing
of hours worked
and rates of pay

calculation of hours worked and
rates of pay

listing of hours worked and rates of
pay (for manual checking)

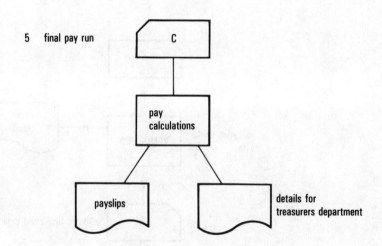

5   final pay run

pay
calculations

payslips

details for
treasurers department

This application is ideal for **batch processing**. Each record is read and processed in turn and the processing could take place at any time convenient to Midshire District Council – possibly at night.

Midshire's employees were widely scattered throughout the District, often in an unpredictable way so that it was impossible to introduce a **clocking-in** system (see question 5). Information about the hours which employees had worked was therefore produced on **timesheets**. The system flowchart in Figure 10.2 describes the five separate stages of the initial Midshire payroll system.

The **rating application** was much superior to **repetitive** and **time-consuming** manual calculation, but a major problem had quickly developed: the processing was too slow.

The Council met at the end of February to set the rate, which became payable on the first of April, so all the rate demand notices had therefore to be printed **within this period**. In order to achieve this target, the system had to be worked 24 hours a day solely on that task. In addition, the system was insufficiently flexible in coping with changes in rateable value caused by, for example, home extensions, change of usage or change of ownership.

Shortly before John's appointment – in an effort to overcome these problems – the Council voted to use the local University mainframe computer for its rating operation. The University, in effect, acted as a **computer bureau**.

Magnetic disc files of the standing information (relatively unchanging detail) had been set up from the punched cards. **Transaction files** of the ratepayers payments, changes of ownership, usage etc. were prepared on a compatible floppy disc based computer at Midshire District Hall and sent to the University at the end of each week. Updating the records was a **batch process** (see p.110).

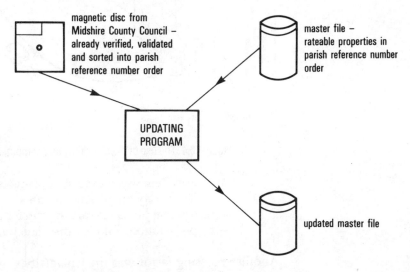

magnetic disc from Midshire County Council – already verified, validated and sorted into parish reference number order

master file – rateable properties in parish reference number order

UPDATING PROGRAM

updated master file

Figure 10.3 Updating the rate records

The University was responsible for the printing of the rate demand notices. In addition, a visual display unit (VDU) connected directly to the mainframe via a private telephone line had been installed at the Town Hall to enable rate queries to be answered.

John was deeply concerned at this situation on a number of counts:

Try question 1 before reading the next section.

(i) The original punch-card hardware at District Hall was desperately in need of replacement.

(ii) There was a serious time lapse between payments and/or variations and updating the computer files. This was due not only to the method of data preparation at District Hall, but also to the computer operation at the University; they were now acting as a bureau for several Councils in similar positions, with consequent delays to each user.

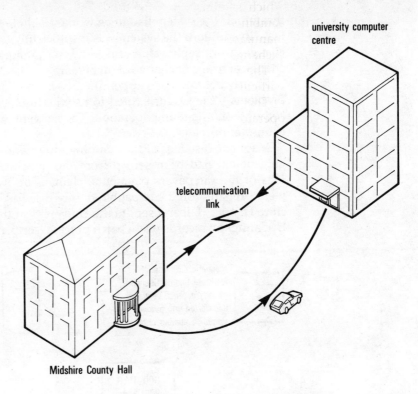

Figure 10.4 The use of the University as a computer bureau

(iii) The system was messy; it now involved three processes:
—the University mainframe for rates
—the original punched-card system for payroll
—the preparation of floppy disc data transaction files.

Another pressing factor was the University's recent decision to raise its bureau charges.

Despite these problems, the necessity for a computer system could not be questioned. For many years the rating system had been so complex – particularly with complicated rate relief systems – that a return to manual methods was impossible.

John wanted to rationalize completely the present arrangements.

Try question 2 before reading the next section.

It would require the purchaser of a modern **mini-computer** with sufficient capacity for both payroll and rate system demands.

After careful consideration he selected a system offering 256 Kbytes of main storage and 15 Mbytes of disc storage (on interchangeable packs, though these were rarely removed). It would also support six VDU workstations on a multi-access operating system. This system had also been selected by three neighbouring Councils – a factor which significantly influenced John's decision. Not only did their combined purchasing power provide a good bargaining base with the manufacturers, but there were also the added advantages of software exchange and local support in case of computer failure.

The first operation to be transferred to the new system was the particularly cumbersome **payroll process**.

The old data preparation system was replaced by a single VDU operator in the payroll section keying in the timesheet data, using a

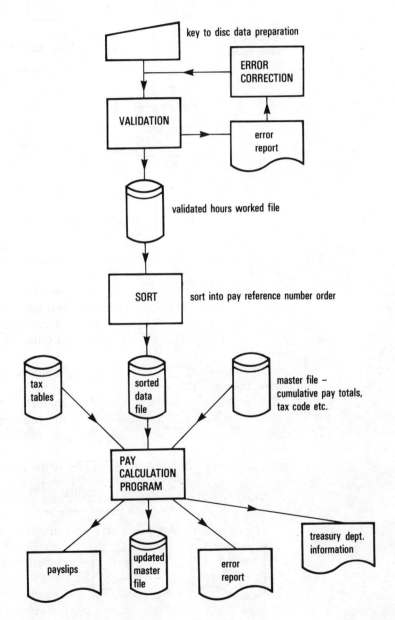

Figure 10.5 Midshire's modern payroll system

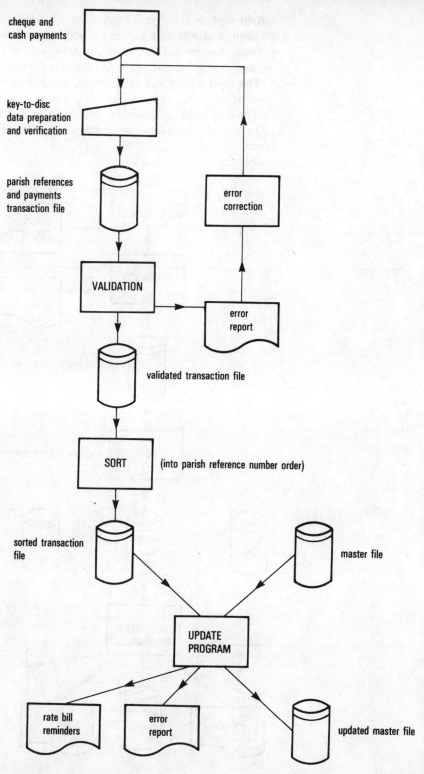

Figure 10.6 Paying the rates

key-to-disc operation. **Verification** was provided by a second data preparation clerk. The system was also now able to incorporate tax tables; these **have** to be held on disc for rapid location of the tax payable for a particular gross pay and tax code.

The time scale for the complete operation was greatly reduced and personnel were released for other tasks. The complete system is shown in Figure 10.5.

Two of the VDU workstations were sited in the rates and rebates offices. Their interactive operation, using a direct access master file, enabled status enquiries to be answered immediately. Similarly, there was now excellent flexibility to cope with change of rateable value, ownership or usage. All these facilities appeared on a menu of options whenever a specific ratepayer's record was located or – for larger numbers of amendments – a transaction file was prepared and run in conjunction with the master file and an upgrade program.

The majority of rate payments were made by post and credited to the ratepayer's account by the system described in Figure 10.6, which is typical of many large-scale billing operations.

The production of the rate demands was also streamlined, with the updating of the Council records for each ratepayer and the printing of the rate demand notices being accomplished in a single operation. Output was on special continuous paper, complete with the name and address, ready to be inserted in a 'window' envelope after being guillotined into individual demands.

Figure 10.7 Production of rate demand notices

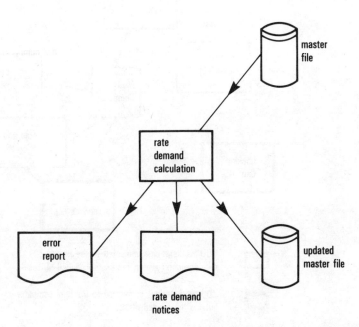

John was extremely pleased with the system, but by 1985 increased demands arising from the **complexity of rating**, **wordprocessing** and

spreadsheet development culminated in the system being 97 per cent full at peak usage.

The success of the word processing software, in particular, had strengthened departmental demand for access to the system. It enabled the operator to compose **standard letters** (or contracts) from stored paragraphs and to insert or superimpose special conditions or individual specifications. The personnel department, for instance, constructed all new contracts of employment in this way. The names and addresses of the recipients were drawn from the main files.

In addition, the District Council expects the computer to play a more significant role in its financial operations as more and more ratepayers choose to pay their rates as a series of direct debit transfers from their bank accounts.

It was decided to upgrade the system to support up to twenty VDU workstations simultaneously with 1 Mbyte of main storage and a 25-Mbyte Winchester. Figure 10.8 below shows the most recent deployment of the Midshire District Council computer system.

Figure 10.8 The final configuration of the Midshire District Council system

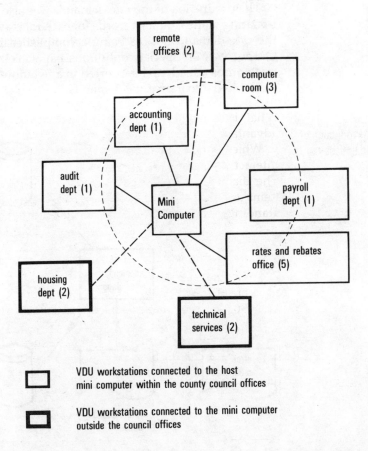

The system also includes two line printers in the computer room and a number of slave printers at particular workstations. A dual floppy

disc drive is also incorporated and has been used extensively in the development of the wordprocessing system.

SUMMARY:		
	1	The complexity of rating systems is now such that it could no longer function without the employment of computers; this is a characteristic shared by an increasing number of services.
	2	Payroll and rating applications are ideal for computerization because they require a large number of repetitive calculations.
	3	The installation of a computer system may not be a 'once-and-for-all' operation.

QUESTIONS – CASE STUDY 1

1   Place yourself in John's position – make a list of any problems which could arise from the Council's present arrangements.
2   Decide what action you would take to rationalize the situation.
3   Why is each ratepayer given a Parish reference number?
4   Describe any validation checks which could be used to ensure the correct transposition of the reference number during processing.
5   In the initial payroll system it was found that a clocking-in system was impractical. How would this have helped?
6   What is a computer bureau? What are its advantages and disadvantages to the customer?
    Which part of Midshire's arrangement with the University allowed interactive operation?
7   The diagram below shows a Midshire rate demand notice. Which items are printed at the time the notice is produced? Which items are standing details and which are calculated during processing?

MIDSHIRE DISTRICT COUNCIL

General rates for the year commencing the 1st April 1987 are enclosed. Payment of the sum shown below is now due but it may be made as a series of ten instalments.

Mr & Mrs J Turner,
10 Orchard Close,
Winterstone.

Reference No. 1236874321Z
Property: House and Garage
Rateable Value: £435
Rate in the £: 140p

SUM DUE   £609

---

8   The system flowchart below shows a simplified updating system. Copy the diagram and use each of the terms below to complete it.
    Transaction file, error report, update program, sort program,

sorted transaction file, validated transaction file, master file, updated master file, error correction, validation.

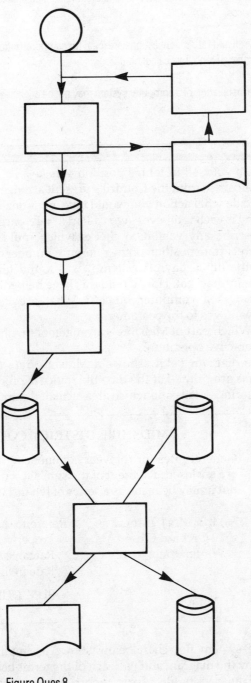

Figure Ques 8

9 At the end of each working day the entire contents of the Winchester disc is 'dumped' to magnetic tape – why?

10 The wordprocessing system is used to compose 'standard' letters. What does 'standard' mean in this context?

11 How do you think Midshire CC used the spreadsheet?

DEVONBRIDE

Sandy was keen to start her own business. After considering several ideas, she concluded that a local 'gap in the market' existed for wedding-dress hire.

Wedding dresses, she reasoned, were extremely – even prohibitively – expensive and only worn once and for a few hours. Conversations with friends and the availability of many dresses for sale second-hand convinced her; she was confident that a good range of virtually new in-fashion dresses could be quickly established for a fraction of their retail cost. Initially, she decided to run the business from home.

This confidence proved to be well-founded. An impressive stock of almost thirty dresses – many of which had never been worn – was rapidly created. Advertising was expensive but worthwhile; many of the dresses were quickly hired.

Each dress was identified by a unique **code**. Sandy decided to make the code a combination of the basic details which she needed – the hire charge, the dress's size and its relative time of purchase within that size. This is illustrated in the figure below.

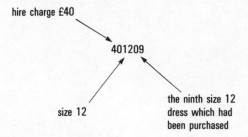

Figure 10.9 Dress coding

At first the dates on which the dresses were hired were entered in a large business diary and on a master wall-chart, but as the stock of dresses expanded, these methods proved inadequate. They were replaced by a separate diary for each dress; this system was effective but cumbersome. Customers who were getting married at relatively short notice frequently wanted to know which garments were available and not to waste their time looking at dresses only to find that they were unavailable. This meant looking in all the diaries.

After some thought, Sandy decided that a microcomputer and

appropriate **information storage and retrieval software** was the solution. She had enjoyed a limited introduction to computers at college and knew, therefore, that she would require a **floppy disc** based system; but she did not have the expertise to write her own software. An **applications package** would be required.

The first stage was to write down what she would ideally like the system to do.

Try question 1 before continuing.

She required it to:

1   **Store the basic details of each dress** (currently held on record cards): its date of purchase, cost, size, reference number and the hire charge.
2   **Store the dates on which each dress was hired.** Experience already suggested that five dates would be ample for this purpose.

The record for each dress would therefore contain ten fields – each field to contain a single item of data – and the complete set of records formed the file. A typical record, she envisaged, would have the structure shown in Figure 10.10.

Reference Number	
Date of Purchase	
Cost	
Size	
Hire Charge	
DATE 1	
DATE 2	
DATE 3	
DATE 4	
DATE 5	

Figure 10.10 A dress record

3   **Have good editing facilities.** One of the main purposes of the system would be to answer customer enquiries as conveniently and swiftly as possible. It would be important that the dates on the records could be easily amended: **inserted** on the formation of a new contract, **deleted** on the completion of a contract and, for added convenience, the software should be capable of **sorting** the dates into calendar order.
4   Be able **to sort** any specified field – e.g. in order of their cost – for periodical analysis.
5   Finally, the records must be easily created and able to be individually displayed.

Sandy realized that the information storage and retrieval packages which she recalled from college did not meet these specifications. Certainly the records had been easy to create. The software, she remembered, simply asked her to name each field, to define the maximum field length and to provide the complete file with a title. Each record was then presented in turn for completion.

```
Reference . . . . . . . . . . .  401207
Purchase  . . . . . . . . . . .  120487
Cost  . . . . . . . . . . . . . .  80
Size . . . . . . . . . . . . . . .  16
Charge . . . . . . . . . . . . .  35
DATE 1 . . . . . . . . . . . .  160687
DATE 2 . . . . . . . . . . . .  200787
DATE 3. . . . . . . . . . . . .
DATE 4 . . . . . . . . . . . .
DATE 5 . . . . . . . . . . . .
```

record headings   details input
generated by the   from the keyboard
software   to create the
                         records

Figure 10.11 Record completion

However, the **interrogation** of the file was limited. Only one field at a time could be interrogated; therefore when a customer wanted to know which dresses were available on a certain date, each date field had to be individually addressed. For instance, to determine the dresses available for hire (by identifying those already hired) on 12 June 1987, a statement similar to the one below was required:

Inquiry * DATE1=120687 OR DATE2=120687 OR DATE3=120687 OR DATE4=120687 OR DATE5=120687

This was still faster than using all the diaries, but it was not what Sandy really required – she **really** wanted a general statement:

Inquiry * DATE*=120687

which would instruct the system to search **all the date fields** of each record. In addition, the sort routines were rather long-winded.

What she actually needed next was expert advice on the availability of software to match her specifications, and its cost.

It quickly emerged that the **operating system** of the hardware which she purchased would have to be PC/DOS compatible – the college microcomputers had been based on the 6502 chip and therefore unable to run the extensive range of IBM compatible business software. The cost of the computer, with its inbuilt 3.5″ twin disc drives, was to be approximately £1,600. This was a significant step for her fledgling business but nevertheless she accepted the dealer's special offer of a two-month limited cost trial.

The records were easy to create and she began by transferring all her record cards – holding basic details of the dresses – and existing bookings on to the computer file. For a time new bookings were recorded in both the diaries and on the computer file (**parallel running**) but before the end of the trial period she had become so confident with the computer system that the diaries had been discarded. She was committed to the purchase of the system and convinced of its advantages:

1 Telephone enquiries on the range of dresses available for a particular date could be quickly answered.

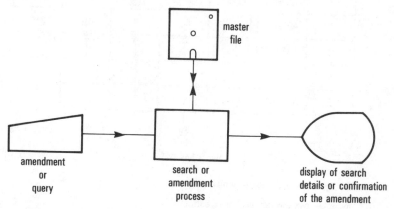

Figure 10.12 Interrogating the system

2 The flexibility of sorting the hire dates for each dress within the record then enabled her to sort on DATE1 across the records to generate the sequence in which the dresses were hired.

3 Analysis by cost of purchase was greatly facilitated.

System enhancement
Sandy decided to purchase further additions to her system:

Try question 2 before continuing.

1 **A word processing chip and a printer.** (Try question 6.)
2 **A spreadsheet.**

Many of Sandy's letters were the same – thanking her customers for payments, writing to confirm details or to refund the damage repair deposits. She always typed the letters individually because she thought that the 'personal' element of the contact was particularly important. It was tiresome but worthwhile. However, with a word-processing system **the standard letters could be stored on disc and personalized at the time of dispatch.**

Sandy wanted to use a spreadsheet so as to gain a clear overall financial picture of her business.

A spreadsheet consists of a grid (letters across, numbers down) of 'boxes'. Each box may contain **text**, **a figure** or a **formula**. The use of a spreadsheet would enable her not only to analyse the current situation but also modify her hire charges (for instance in line with inflation) and view the overall effect: the **'what if?'** situation. This is illustrated in Figure 10.13.

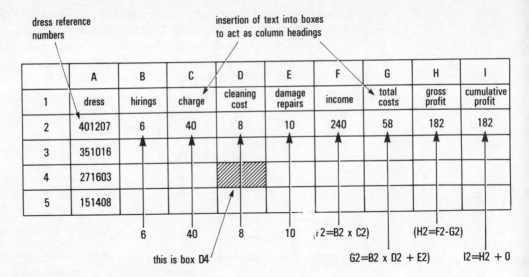

dress reference numbers

insertion of text into boxes to act as column headings

	A	B	C	D	E	F	G	H	I
1	dress	hirings	charge	cleaning cost	damage repairs	income	total costs	gross profit	cumulative profit
2	401207	6	40	8	10	240	58	182	182
3	351016								
4	271603			/////					
5	151408								

6   40   8   10   (F2=B2 x C2)   (H2=F2-G2)

this is box D4   G2=B2 x D2 + E2)   I2=H2 + 0

the figures show the actual display

the actual box contents may mave been generated by formulas

check that the formulas actually give the details shown

Figure 10.13 Spreadsheet

THE FUTURE

The success of the business enabled Sandy to acquire shop premises in the town and also to expand her business by moving into the sale of wedding dresses as well as their hire. The purchase of the PC/DOS compatible computer proved to be a particular bonus here, as she was able to purchase **stock control software** without difficulty.

Further progress soon permitted the opening of a second shop. Sandy installed a similar basic computer system in the new shop but added a **modem**; this enabled the system to communicate with the first (host); therefore information on the total stock was readily available to both shops.

QUESTIONS – CASE STUDY 2

1   Place yourself in Sandy's position. Write down the ideal capabilities of the system.
2   What additional facilities would you advise Sandy to purchase?
3   What is the key field for each record?
4   What would be the reference number of the twelfth size 10 dress which Sandy had purchased if its hire charge was £35?
5   Decode the dress reference number 451506.
6   Why is the maximum field length specified?

7   A customer selects a particular dress and asks Sandy to determine its
    availability. Describe how Sandy would use her computer system to
    respond to the customer's request.

8   Describe how Sandy would find out which dresses were available for
    a particular date.

9   Why do you think Sandy has specified a twin disc drive system?

10 What is meant by parallel running in the context of the the introduc-
    tion of a new computer system?

11 What type of printer do you think Sandy will purchase to complete
    her word processing system?

12 This question refers to Figure 10.13. What will the boxes F4 and G4
    actually contain?

COMPUTER APPLICATIONS

CONTENTS

The range of computer applications today is vast, and increasing all the time. The purpose of this chapter is not to enumerate even a small percentage of those applications, but to illustrate the general principles characterizing problems which are suitable for the application of computer techniques, by reference to specific examples.

When answering applications questions, two important points should be remembered.

1 **Read the question very carefully and pay particular attention to the marks which are available for each section.** This is vital examination technique throughout the papers, but is especially relevant to applications questions, which are frequently divided into sections.

   The marks for each section provide a clear guide to the length or detail expected by the examiners and the number of separate points which the answer to that section must contain: one point – one mark. If, for instance, there is only one mark available for suggesting an input device, no further credit will be obtained from a detailed comparison of the advantages and disadvantages of several devices which might be appropriate – however excellent the argument! Similarly, if asked to state the advantages of a system there will be little point point in criticizing it.

2 In the discussion of a system **use a clearly structured approach** which considers each stage. Examiners look to award marks – a clearly structured solution or answer will help them in this task!

   Input. How is the data captured? Is it encoded? How is it transmitted to the CPU?

   Process. What computing takes place? What is the computer actually doing?

   Storage. Does the system use backing storage? If so, which? Why is this the most appropriate?

   Output. What is the output method? Why? Is hard copy required (using special stationery)? Is speed an important factor? Why?

   In addition, a **global view** of the system is important. What are its advantages over the system which it replaced? Are there any disadvantages?

   We already know that computer applications may be broadly divided into three types: **real time**, **interactive** and **batch processes**.

The fundamental characteristic of real-time applications is the response of the computer system in real time; any delay is of **vital** importance.

A specific example is the **control of a chemical process** which must take place within defined limits of pressure, temperature or other measurable variables.

INPUT

Input to the system uses pressure and temperature sensors. Their readings are input directly to the computer via analogue to digital converters.

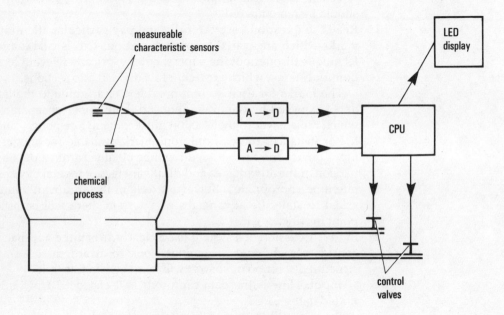

Figure 11.1 Chemical process control system

PROCESS

The CPU compares the readings with the pre-defined limits. If the readings are within the limits, no action is taken. If the readings fall outside the limits, the computer adjusts the valves which control the measurable characteristics. This is the **feedback principle**. The results of any changes by the computer are fed back to it as the sampling continues. The rate of sampling will vary with the application, but it will be many times a second.

STORAGE

While the control process itself requires no backing storage (the current temperature and pressure readings along with their pre-defined limits will be held in the main store), the values of the measurable characteristics will be dumped to magnetic disc at set intervals dependent on the application; this is an example of **data-logging**.

OUTPUT

The most important output of the system is the control process, but in addition an LED (light emitting diode) display will be available to enable the operator to monitor the system.

The use of a real-time computer system to control chemical processes permits much more precise control of the measurable characteristics which are involved. Human operators could not monitor the process with the same frequency or make small adjustments to the valves with the same unerring accuracy. In addition, the computer system is never tired or distracted.

In some real-time control applications, such as the most recent generation of flight training simulators, human beings could not hope to perform the array of complex calculations at the speed required for realistic simulation.

Where industrial processes – such as the chemical process above, or steel rolling mills – or vital public services such as air traffic control or automatic railway signalling are **dependent** on real-time computing, a **back-up system is essential**.

Normally this will involve a second computer **running in parallel** with the first – that is, receiving all the data and performing exactly as if it were the controlling computer. In the event of a breakdown, the second computer would take over from the first automatically, with no processing interruption. It would also be used during routine maintenance of the primary computer. Some systems may also incorporate a **third computer on standby** and an **alternative power supply** which cuts in automatically at times of mains supply failure.

The failsafe requirement of all real-time systems is safety. In the event of an uncontrollable emergency the system will be programmed to make the process safe. In a chemical process, for instance, all valves would be set to a safe position; for automatic railway signalling, all signals would be set to stop. Finally, all systems will include a manual override option to provide manual control in the event of a complete computer system breakdown.

INTERACTIVE COMPUTING

Interactive computing can be recognized by the 'dialogue' which takes place between the user and the computer system.

BANK CASHPOINT

The **bank cashpoint** has already been quoted as an example of this mode of operation, and because of the increasing availability of this facility we will examine the application in greater detail.

INPUT

Input to the system is from two sources:

(*a*)   **The customer's cashpoint card.** This contains his name and account number encoded on its magnetic stripe; it enables the cashpoint terminal to access his account record in the main computer files. The insertion of the card also triggers the withdrawal of any terminal protection screen preventing unauthorized access to the terminal keypad.

(*b*)   **The special cashpoint terminal keypad** which the customer uses to key in his PIN – personal identification number.

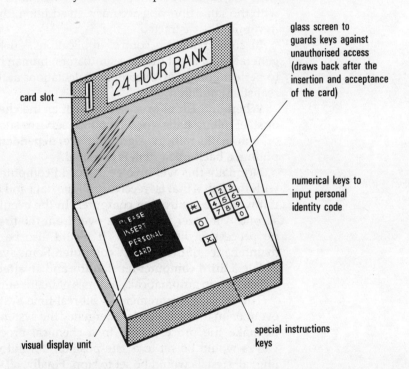

Figure 11.2 Cashpoint terminal

PROCESS

The PIN keyed in by the customer and that on his account record are compared by the computer. If they do not match, the customer will be offered two further opportunities to key in the correct code; after this the system will retain the card and cease functioning. If the PINs match, the customer will be offered a range of services. The most popular is the withdrawal of cash, but a customer could also obtain the balance of his account, request a full statement or transfer funds between his accounts.

STORAGE

The bank account files are stored at its main office on **magnetic discs** to provide rapid access to individual accounts. The central computer and cashpoint terminal are connected by private telephone lines and, in some cases, the data transmissions are scrambled for greater security. The customer's account will be debited by the amount which he has withdrawn at the time of the transaction and a separate record of all transactions at the terminal will be maintained (see Figure 5.11).

OUTPUT

Usually cash! But it could also be LCD (liquid crystal display) showing the customer's balance or confirming his statement request.

Bank cashpoints are of real benefit to the customer. They provide a comprehensive service 24 hours a day. From the bank's point of view, their provision attracts customers and they offer a cheaper service than cashiers; a significant fall in banking staff is predicted as the paper generated by financial transactions is gradually reduced.

Cashpoints are only one aspect of the enormous deployment of computers in the financial sector.

CHEQUE HANDLING

The use of MICR on bank cheques is described on p.28.

At the end of each day all the cheques which have been cashed are sent to the Banks Automatic Clearance System (BACS) in London, where they are **sorted** (using the magnetic ink characters) and returned to the account-holder branches. In addition a program is run each night which updates the balances in all the accounts where transactions have taken place and provides a physical record on **microfiche** for each branch.

STATEMENTS

Computers are also used to produce statements of customer accounts at agreed intervals. The name and address of the customer, drawn by the computer from his file, is automatically printed on to the statement so that the document can be placed in a 'window' envelope ready for posting.

THE CASHLESS SOCIETY

The basis of the 'cashless' society is EFTPOS (electronic funds transfer at the point of sale). In essence, a direct link between a shop or supermarket computer and the customer's bank computer would enable cash settlement of the bill to be made immediately by adding the appropriate amount to the shop's account and deducting it from the customer's account. Despite a number of experiments, both in this country and abroad, there are as yet no indications that this system will become widespread. Its advantages to the customer are unclear, but it may have several potential drawbacks. The system enables a check to be made which ensures that the customer has sufficient funds to pay the bill and this may cause some embarrassment. Also, the cash is transferred **immediately**, which may disadvantage customers normally paying by cheque; in addition, there are potential security problems arising from the loss or theft of the plastic card.

A more promising 'next step' is the wider availability of SMART cards. These cards are not merely cheque support or cashpoint cards – they are cash. These cards can be both read from and written to, rather like British Telecom phonecards. The are purchased for an initial face value and, as they are used, the value of the purchase is deducted from the remaining balance. They can be used repeatedly until completely spent.

The electronic transfer of funds on a commercial level is already firmly established. Within Britain the bank computers are linked using the PSS system (see p.131), and internationally the SWIFT network (Society for Worldwide Interbank Financial Telecommunications) is used extensively.

BATCH PROCESSING

In a batch process, data with a common processing requirement is grouped and run in a single operation. Time is not usually a vital issue in batch processes; its main advantages are:

(*a*)   **cost** – it is a relatively cheap processing system;

(*b*)   **convenience** – processing can be done when other system demands are low.

The payroll system used by Midshire County Council in Chapter 10 is a batch process (a common example of this type of processing), as is cheque handling by the clearing banks. We will examine a third, increasingly common, example – **the ordering of meals by hospital patients**.

HOSPITAL MEALS

INPUT

Each morning the patients complete a card similar to the one shown below. It contains the menu for the evening meal and the patient's choice is indicated by placing a pencil mark in the appropriate space. The complete set of cards is then gathered together (batched) and input to the computer using **OMR**.

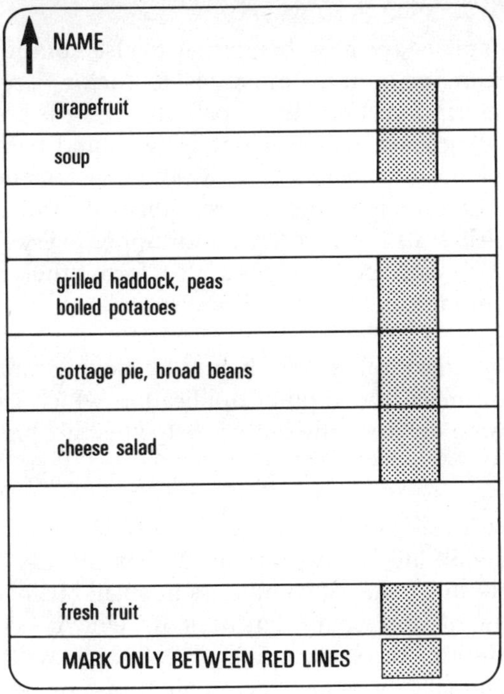

Figure 11.3 Menu card

PROCESS

The total requirement for each menu choice is computed along with the total ingredients that this will require.

STORAGE

As the data is read, it is stored on a Winchester for later statistical analysis.

OUTPUT

Hard copy of the total number of patients requiring each choice and a complete list of ingredients and quantities which must be purchased – a shopping list.
This system minimizes the length of time ahead of which the patient must order his meals. It also reduces the wastage of food; because the meal for which the patients are ordering is only a short time ahead they are confident that they will eat the meal which they order and this makes the system very cost effective.

GENERAL HOSPITAL APPLICATIONS

Hospitals are now beginning to use computer systems not only to streamline administrative tasks, doctors' appointment lists, printing prescriptions and labels, patients' records and stock control, but also in **diagnosis**, using **expert systems** and **patient care**. **Intensive care systems**, for instance, allow the constant monitoring of a patient's condition – his temperature, pulse rate and other measurable characteristics. In the severely handicapped, very limited degrees of movement can be exploited to form the basis of computerized communication or mobility systems.

We will complete this chapter by looking more briefly at other important areas of computer application which might be readily used by examiners or by the candidate to illustrate his answers.

SMALL BUSINESS APPLICATIONS

Devonbride, in case study 2, has already drawn attention to the potential value of computers in small businesses. This is particularly true of any small business to which sales accounts (VAT), re-ordering, record keeping or extensive written communications are essential, e.g. small car repair firms, owner-occupied shops, estate agents. One such application is dairy farming.

Dairy farming

Modern dairy farming requires considerable capital investment in both machinery and food concentrate. The important figure to the farmer is the amount by which the yield of the cow (in cash) is greater than its cost (in terms of the food which it eats). Use of a computer system enables the individual cow to be constantly monitored.

Figure 11.4 Typical printout from a dairy farm system

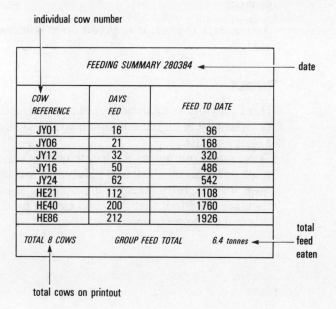

Each cow is identified to the system either by **keyboard input** or a **transponder**, which emits a unique identifying signal. Its milk yield can then be **individually** monitored. The use of computerized systems has shown that average profit margins of £450 per cow have disguised real profit margins between £300 and £800. The herd records will be **updated** each milking session; many systems also incorporate **a printer** for additional convenience (see question 2).

In addition, the milk production of each cow is closely related to its food intake. In automated feeding systems the cow's identifying transponder will trigger the computer to provide the precise amount of feed concentrate required for that individual cow.

ROBOTS

These are now firmly established in manufacturing industry, e.g. car manufacture. They operate either by continuously repeating a preprogrammed sequence of instructions or under the direct control of a computer program employing the **feedback principle**; the latter is an example of a real-time control process.

In addition to being able to operate in hazardous environments and to perform tasks inappropriate to human beings – e.g. 'sniffer' robots in car manufacture are used to sniff gases which would indicate leaks in the rubber weather seals of a car – robots are also able to function continuously over lengthy periods.

This latter characteristic is now bringing fully mechanized milking closer to reality. Cows do not like to be milked twice a day – this is the standard routine because it is realistic in terms of manpower. Experiments are now taking place which would enable cows to enter the milking parlour whenever they wished to be milked; the robot could work 24 hours a day, with very short breaks for cleaning. In addition the cow would be automatically fed with an amount corresponding to its yield, weighed and checked.

WEATHER FORECASTING

The essence of weather forecasting is to measure the variable characteristics of temperature, humidity, air pressure, wind speed, rainfall etc. at frequent intervals (usually twice a day), and to use this information to generate the weather pattern existing at that time. A scientific prediction of future changes in this pattern is then made, in step-by-step fashion, using highly complex **mathematical models**; the stepped patterns can be seen daily on the television weather forecast predictive sequences. Speed in these difficult calculations is essential – a weather forecast is of little use if the predicted weather has already arrived.

The UK Meteorological Office at Bracknell has used computers since 1959. It now has a complex family of interlinked computers. Information is gathered from a variety of sources including:

1   **ground or surface (ships at sea) stations;**
2   **monitoring the controlled release of helium balloons** which transmit data on temperature, humidity and air pressure in digital form;
3   **information from other countries;**
4   **satellite data**; transmitted either from polar orbiting satellites or from geostationary satellites, i.e. satellites which remain in a constant position in relation to the surface of the earth – geostationary satellites are used for data communications.

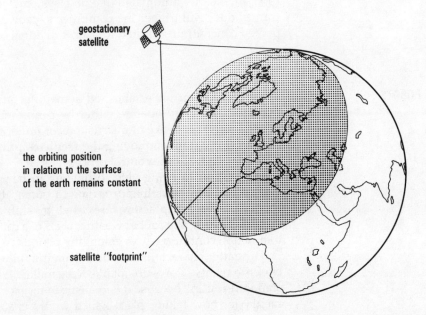

Figure 11.5 Geostationary satellites

All this data is held on magnetic discs and, in addition to the fundamental task of merging it into the predictive calculations, computers are also used to:

(i) prepare pictures from the image data transmitted by satellites and superimpose the coastal outlines;

(ii) produce weather maps complete with isobars and coastal outlines

Prestel is an excellent medium for weather forecast presentation. Special equipment at the weather centre enables the content to be frequently updated to reflect the most recent acquisition of data and consequent predictions.

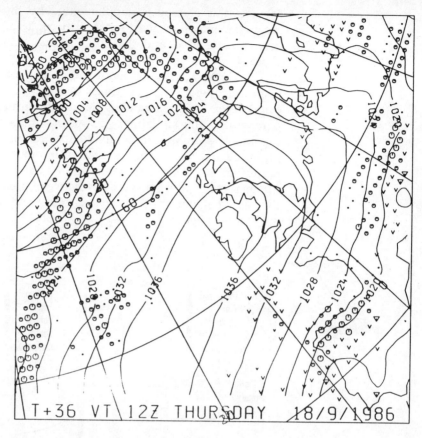

Figure 11.6 A computer generated weather chart produced by the computer system at Bracknell, used for short-range forecasting.

POLICE COMPUTING

Most regional police forces have two computer systems at their disposal:

A LOCAL FORCE COMPUTER SYSTEM

This is used to employ the local resources of that force as efficiently as possible and to maintain local records.

THE POLICE NATIONAL COMPUTER

The PNC is housed at Hendon (North London). It is linked to police forces throughout the UK by approximately 800 terminals. The system uses three Burroughs B7700 central processors which normally work together but can be partitioned into two separate computers for maintenance. A fourth B7800 is used for software development and testing. The magnetic disc capacity of the system exceeds 11,000

Mbytes; this storage is supplemented by thirteen fully automatic magnetic tape drives used for security copies and the transfer of data between the PNC and the DVLC (Driving and Vehicle Licensing Centre).

The importance of maintaining an interruption-free, rapid response operation at all times is not only reflected in the CPU duplication. Many of the PNC files are duplicated, and maintained by parallel real-time updating; special real-time software is used – it is capable of searching for individual words or phrases at **extremely high speeds**. The response time is impressive. A simple enquiry requiring only a short response will be completed in approximately fifteen seconds; the general delay between pressing the send key and the reply beginning is only five seconds, some of which is telecommunications delay.

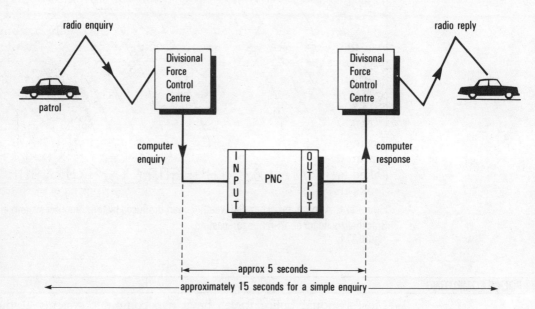

Figure 11.7 Interrogating the PNC

The database of the PNC consists of six main files:

1 **Vehicle owners** – the name and address of the legal owner of every vehicle in the UK. Its entries now exceed 30 million.

2 **Stolen vehicles** – full description, including registration, engine and chassis numbers of all vehicles known to be stolen.

3 **Convicted persons** – the name of all persons convicted of serious crime.

4 **Wanted or missing persons file** – all the people wanted by the police for various reasons.

5 **Fingerprints file** – the coded index of all convicted persons.

6 **Disqualified drivers.**

All this information is **factual** and has always been available to the police. However, shortening the length of time for an enquiry is a significant step in the fight against crime.

Public concern about the police use of computers, which centres on criminal intelligence and file misuse, is considered in more detail in chapter 12. We should note here that, despite the almost complete exemption of the PNC from the Data Protection Act and recent incidents damaging to the image of the Police Force, there has been no large scale public concern targeted on the PNC and no significant or repeated evidence of PNC misuse.

SUPERMARKET SHOPPING

In some early computerized supermarket stock control systems, restocking was an end-of-day task. Each item, identified by its bar code, was recorded on cassette tape along with the number required. The complete order was then transmitted to a central mini-computer over the telephone lines. The central computer collated the group or regional requirements of the supermarket chain, transmitted loading instructions to the warehouse and reorder requests to the manufacturers. At the warehouse goods were loaded overnight and delivered before the start of the following working day.

In more modern systems the deployment of computers varies, but the increasing installation of POS systems allows **sales data to be captured as the sales take place**. Typically each POS terminal is linked to the supermarket's microcomputer. It is this computer which 'looks up' the item description and price corresponding to the bar

Figure 11.8 The POS system.

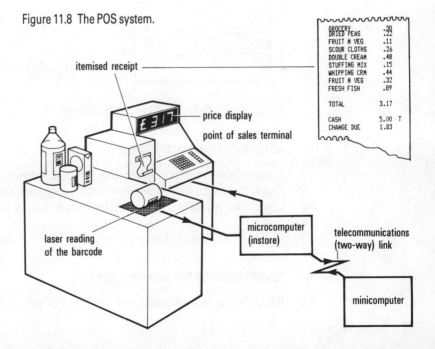

code reading. These details are displayed at the POS terminal and printed on to the customer's receipt.

The microcomputer also records the running totals for the sale of each item and informs the central mini-computer if stock falls below pre-determined levels.

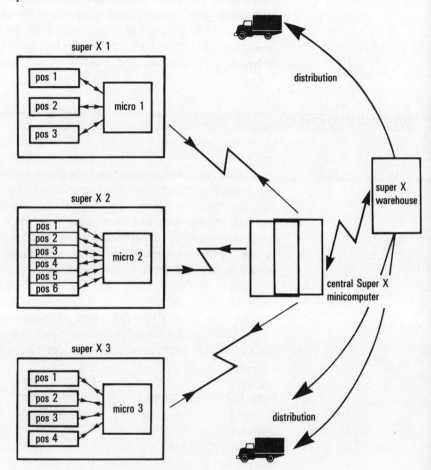

Figure 11.9 Computerized supermarket stock control

ADVANTAGES TO THE CUSTOMER

1 **Queues move faster.** With the possible future adoption of cashless shopping there would be no delays while customers write cheques.
2 **Checkout mistakes are greatly reduced** in comparison with traditional tills.
3 **A detailed, itemized receipt** is much easier for the customer to check.

ADVANTAGES FOR THE MANAGEMENT

1 **Re-ordering is automatic** and, because of this, the traditional need for

a large on-site warehouse is removed – and so is the need to employ warehouse staff. Costs are therefore lowered; these savings can be passed on to the customer, thus attracting more custom.

2   **Accurate sales records are produced.** These enable individual products, selected promotions or seasonal variations to be analysed.

3   **Prices can be quickly altered.** Some cases have already come to light where customers have been charged a different price from that which was displayed. This does little for public confidence in advanced technology. It usually occurs in systems where the POS terminal is connected directly to the central minicomputer and local special offers are incorrectly programmed.

The main disadvantage is the initial high cost of POS systems.

EDUCATION

Computers are now used extensively at all levels of education. The most common application is the use of school microcomputers for interactive **computer aided learning (CAL)**. They may also be used for **simulations** – particularly where the subject matter is too dangerous for normal school experiments – **design work and creative developments**. The extension of microcomputing throughout school and college curricula is now being assisted by the increasing availability of high quality, relatively cheap software.

LIBRARIES

Libraries, including an increasing number of school libraries, are incorporating computerized systems. The standard library card index file details are copied to computer files and supplemented by a brief number of 'key' words 'describing' the book. Traditional library searches to located a specified book by a particular author are readily accommodated, but additionally a **keyword search** can be made; i.e. if the person wants to know which books contain significant references on bridges, a keyword search on 'bridges' will display all the books in the library which feature 'bridges' in their keyword description. This feature is particularly useful in school libraries where coursework research is frequently centred on a **topic** rather than a particular author or books.

In more sophisticated systems, all the library books and library membership cards are labelled with bar codes. Early bar code systems used a bar code reader to create a **transaction file**, on cassette tape, of all the loans and book returns during the day. The master loans file, a complete record of all the books loaned by the library and their borrowers was then updated at the end of each day. In some cases this could mean a 24-hour delay before the system was updated.

Modern systems, often based on central county minicomputers, offer real-time updating and rapid information on books held throughout the county. In the case of a loan, the identifying bar code is read, that book located in the master file, flagged accordingly and the borrower's membership number added to the record. In the case of a returned book, the flag and membership number are removed.

Most libraries within this system have several terminals **permanently connected** to the minicomputer. **Interrogation** of the master file will not only determine which library loaned the book, but also which terminal at that library. At least one terminal will normally be a 'public' terminal which allows members of the general public to interrogate the total library collection and to have up to the minute information as to which books are on loan.

This system greatly improves the maintenance of accurate records. It also provides lists of overdue books and the addition of an **integrated wordprocessing system** would enable the reminders to be printed automatically.

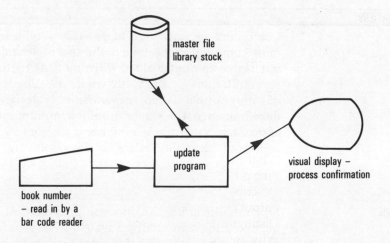

Figure 11.10 Updating the Library Master File

ADMINISTRATION

The value of microcomputers for educational administration is increasingly recognized and their use is now a common feature in many schools. The software for the suite of administrative programs will be **integrated** so that the basic data need only be **keyed in once**; it can then be accessed repeatedly for a variety of applications.

In addition, some authorities are introducing complete LEA (Local Education Authority) administrative systems centred on minicomputers and linking schools throughout the Authority.

SUMMARY:

1   The GCSE examination will look for a general appreciation of the characteristics of tasks appropriate for the application of computer techniques.

2   An understanding of some specific examples of computer applications is essential to illustrate these general principles, but candidates should avoid over-emphasis and in-

depth learning of small operational details – the broad appreciation of a range of applications is much more valuable.

3   Use the mark scheme of a question – it provides a good guide as to the level of detail or length which the chief examiner expects in each section of the question.

4   Use a structured approach in all applications answers: input – process – storage – output and a global summary of the overall advantages and disadvantages of the system.

5   Be prepared to distinguish between the processing requirement of different applications:
— in real-time systems, any delay is crucial. Data capture is usually automatic (analogue to digital conversion); control systems will use the feedback principle.
— in interactive systems the user is on line to the CPU; there is a dialogue between the user and the computer system.
— batch processing systems are relatively cheap and can provide convenient processing; time is not usually a vital factor.

6   Know at least one example of each type of processing in sufficient depth to use in the illustration of your answers, should the opportunity arise.

CHAPTER 11 QUESTIONS

1   What is the feedback principle? Describe how it operates in a real-time processing application.

2   Describe the dairy farming application in terms of input, process, output and storage.

3   Distinguish between real-time processing and interactive processing.

4   Why are magnetic discs the selected method of storage for the cash-point application?

5   Many supermarkets now use product bar codes. Explain how the price of each article is determined from this code. State two advantages for this system in relation to the customer and two in relation to the management.

6   Design a systems flowchart for the older of the two library systems described in this chapter.

7   A certain computer is to be used to monitor temperature levels at intervals of 1 second. It is also to be used to process data previously recorded. Interrupts are to be used to allow both tasks to be performed efficiently.
    Explain what is meant by interrupts, with reference to the above example.   (M)

8   A small firm needs to use a computer system for information retrieval. It can either use a microcomputer with floppy discs or have on-line access to a mainframe computer.
    State one advantage and one disadvantage to the firm if it uses a microcomputer.

9   A library uses a computerized system to record which books have been loaned. When books are loaned the following data is recorded on computer files:

  (i) The borrower's code number;

  (ii) The code numbers of the books which have been borrowed.

(*a*)   Suggest, with a reason, a suitable method of data capture.

(*b*)   State two reasons why code numbers are used rather than book titles.

(*c*)   State one way in which a computerized library might affect the privacy of the borrowers.   (L)

SOCIAL AND ECONOMIC EFFECTS

CONTENTS

Computer systems are now a part of our society. The examining groups will expect candidates to be aware of the significant social and organizational changes. It is particularly important that candidates are able to present a reasoned view of a system, which recognizes both **its positive and negative aspects**.

We have already seen that many of the major tasks which computer systems perform or services which they facilitate would now be impossible without them:

> —**bank cashpoint terminals**
> —**weather forecasting**
> —**travel booking services**
> —**supermarket stock control**
> —**large payroll applications**

On a smaller scale, many consumer products now incorporate microprocessors – a complete CPU on a single chip – to provide greater accuracy, control and reliability:

> —**cameras**
> —**washing machines**
> —**toasters**
> —**digital timers**

Computer systems are being used to develop – even to transform – the lives of individuals, to offer opportunities which would otherwise not be possible:

> —**Telecom Gold offers the opportunity for the deaf to hold a visual conversation (the chat facility)**
> —**the physically handicapped are made more mobile**
> —**new forms of leisure are available**
> —**bus stops 'talk' to the blind using computer controlled voice synthesizers.**

These are only a few examples of the obvious benefits made possible by the development and introduction of computer systems. Other consequences of their introduction provide some contrast. Employment and the use of databases are particularly emotive issues.

It has often been argued that computers cause unemployment and there is no doubt that many **repetitive** jobs have been either replaced or made unnecessary by computer systems; the task of a filing clerk, for instance, is removed by the introduction of a computer system which provides direct access to any record from a series of on-line VDU workstations.

Employers may regard this trend as inevitable if their product is to compete successfully in the world market – the adoption of automated systems by one manufacturer often means that his competitors must adopt similar systems. People are increasingly expensive, not only in terms of their pay but also in the range of benefits to which they are often entitled. Computers and computer-controlled machinery will repeatedly perform their tasks to a defined standard; moreover they will work non-stop to maximize output, if necessary in conditions unsuitable for humans, e.g. in a dust-filled atmosphere.

The impact of computers on employment has been exaggerated by their introduction during a period of (world) economic decline, but even if the jobs return, they will be of a **different character**. Repetitive assembly or commercial processes will be computerized and emphasis will be placed on those **people with skills**. The most significant effect of computers is therefore on the unskilled sector of the job market. The computer industry has itself created jobs for computer personnel (see chapter 12), in component manufacture (e.g. silicon chips and assembly) and in systems maintenance, but these are skilled appointments. The jobs which are being created do not match the limited qualifications or experience of those who are being displaced by the application of computer technology.

In many cases, following the introduction or expansion of computer systems, there are no redundancies. The personnel take early retirement or are re-trained for different tasks, as was the case at Midshire District Council. Overall, while this will often provide a realistic solution for a particular employer, the vacancies which might normally have arisen in that industry are no longer available. This solution also focuses attention on the demands of change produced by the introduction of new technology; a positive attitude from the whole workforce towards **re-training and the acquisition of new skills**, throughout their working lives, is a vital cornerstone of future manufacturing and commercial prosperity. The training itself may use computer technology to a greater extent in the future, with the application of interactive video techniques allowing each person to learn at their own pace.

The introduction of computer technology often crosses **traditional craft or skill boundaries** and sometimes the requirement for these skills is completely removed. A well-publicized illustration of this situation lies in newspaper production. Traditionally, journalists typed their contribution; it then had to be cast in lead by a typesetter and composed into pages by the compositor before the printing plates could be made. In advanced computer systems journalists key their work directly into the computer (or transmit it from a remote point). The computer then composes the newspaper pages and drives a laser to produce the printing plates.

But the employment picture is not all gloom. Jobs **assisted** by high technology are frequently more interesting because they provide greater variety. A word processor operator, for instance, will often find more job satisfaction than a typist.

The adoption of new communication techniques, including electronic mail, may **vastly reduce the need for travel** and for the creation of a central workplace – often reached and left by a tedious journey and expensive to maintain. Similarly, the use of computer technology can provide employment opportunities for those compelled to remain at home because of family or disability factors. Any significant increase in working from home will, however, have to be accompanied by a more general recognition of this practice as real work – some experiments involving company executives working from home have revealed a 'loss of status' felt by the executives because of the reaction of friends and colleagues. Another danger is the possible isolation of the worker.

If the increasing application of computers is a competitive necessity, then the government and unions must seek to ensure that society as a whole benefits. The wealth of the nation **will be created by fewer people** and it may well be that such schemes as job-sharing require urgent development. It is a significant problem that the status of a person in society is largely determined by his job. Computer technology can bring massive benefits, including the provision of greater leisure time for everybody, if its introduction is carefully planned and implemented.

THE USE OF DATABASES

A database is a collection of structured data which may be used for more than one application. It will normally consist of **several** files under the software control of a database management system (DBMS) which will allow cross referral for a specific application. The Police National Computer (PNC) is an example of a database.

Public concern has developed because of their use in the storage and retrieval of **personal data**. The debate has centred on three factors – the privacy, security and integrity of data.

PRIVACY

The need for privacy – the right of the individual to keep aspects of his personal life confidential – has been highlighted by the receipt of unsolicited mail targeted at sections of the population, e.g. financial advice from companies who **know** that a person has just retired; and the fear of some individuals that particular details of the distant past may affect their future, e.g. a short prison sentence.

SECURITY

The taking of measures to ensure that there is no unauthorized access is the recognition of privacy.

Security for the actual files will include the measures detailed on p.87.

Security against **unauthorized access** will include:
1 **restricting access** to the computer room (and keeping it locked!);
2 **keeping file names secret**;
3 **using passwords**.

If a password is used, the computer may be programmed to respond to a number of different words which indicate increased levels of responsibility and therefore provide access to greater amounts of – or more sensitive – data. Alternatively only limited password holders may be permitted to write to the file, as opposed to reading its contents. The use of passwords will also enable a **computer log** to be maintained of the personnel who have accessed particular records.

INTEGRITY

This lies in the accuracy of the data. It is a particularly emotive issue and attention is periodically drawn to it by isolated incidents which reveal the storage of incorrect data. Some incidents have involved retailers refusing customers credit arrangements; in rare cases, their decisions were based on false data.

The measures taken to guard against inaccurate data may include:
1 **typing the data twice**;
2 **range checks** on the input data;
3 a system of **check digits**;
4 the use of **write permit rings** on magnetic tapes; the tape can only be written to if the removable write permit ring is in place;
5 providing each data subject (person) with an **accurate record of the details** held in the database.

The potential misuse of databases was first recognized by the government in 1972 with the commissioning of the Younger Committee to investigate the need for legislation to protect the individual citizen. Its main recommendation – that databases should be licensed and registered – and the basic principles of the Data Protection Committee (1978) are found in the Data Protection Act.

THE DATA PROTECTION ACT

This Act, somewhat belated in terms of similar steps taken much earlier by other nations, was passed in 1984 and becomes fully effective in November 1987. It required all data users – public bodies or private companies who control and use personal data – to register by 11 May 1986.

The Act protects **privacy** by requiring all data to be held only for specified purposes and used solely for those purposes. The data must be accurate (**integrity**) and available for inspection by the data subject. The data must also be protected from unauthorized access, alteration, accidental loss or deliberate destruction (**security**). In addition, the Act states that the data must be obtained fairly (data suppliers are not to be misled), that the data cannot be excessive for its purpose (sufficient and no more) and that it must not be kept for longer than necessary.

The Act is designed to protect the rights of the individual. It will also allow the government to ratify the Council of Europe Convention on Data Protection; failure to comply with its conditions would have prevented Britain from being a full partner in the electronic storage and transmission of data, which could have had serious financial and trading implications.

While there is some concern that the Act does not include a compulsory procedure requiring data users to inform data subjects that personal data is being held and describing the arrangements for its inspection, the main area of controversy is possibly the exemption of data held for the purposes of preventing or detecting crime. This exemption may in effect provide police, tax and immigration authorities with complete immunity from the provisions of the Act.

Furthermore, this legislation is unlikely to limit the activities of many computer 'hackers' who regard breaking into the personal records of a database as a challenge. In some cases – such as the trial of Steven Gold and Robert Schifreen in 1986 (for breaking into the Prestel system) – their activities draw attention to the need for improved security measures. The susceptibility of electronic data transfer to 'eavesdropping' from remote electronic devices has also been clearly demonstrated. Where data is particularly sensitive, it must be extensively protected, as in the case of the **Tempest standard** which protects data transfer within the NATO (North Atlantic Treaty Organization) alliance. Computer crime is a **major concern** of large financial institutions who regularly move enormous sums of money by electronic transfer. The characteristics of computer assisted theft may differ from those of 'normal' theft; it may not, for instance, be a single act but a vast number of extremely small occurrences – possibly unnoticed by the individual but very significant in total. Such crimes can be extremely difficult to detect. Some cases of fraud or theft have come to the attention of the public but it is thought that others, possibly a much greater number, have been suppressed for fear that the public may lose confidence in the institution or bank concerned.

The pace of change over the past decade has been dramatic in terms of the application of computer technology. Only now is the legislative process beginning to catch up and to prescribe acceptable public standards.

SUMMARY:

1 Computers are now an essential part of our society.

2 Many of the tasks which they perform would be impossible without them.

3 The changes made by computer technology are not all on a large scale. Many household consumer items now employ microprocessors for greater reliability and control.

4 The most significant change brought by computer systems in terms of employment is a reduction in the number of unskilled jobs which are available and their partial replacement by skilled opportunities.

5 Where the introduction of computer technology cuts across traditional skill or trade boundaries there may be major problems – particularly if the trade union is well organized and redundancies likely – but this is not inevitable where both sides adhere to a firm principle of negotiation.

6 A positive attitude to re-training and the acquisition of new skills throughout a career is essential.

7 Jobs aided by computer technology are often made more interesting by their variety.

8 The planned introduction of computer technology may enable the wealth of the nation to be generated by a smaller number of man-hours. Greater leisure time could thus be available to the whole population.

9 A database is a collection of structured data used for more than one application.

10 Individuals who permit personal data to be stored expect privacy, security and integrity of data.

11 The Data Protection Act protects the rights of individuals (data subjects) on whom data users hold personal information.

12 Computer crime, including theft, hacking and electronic eavesdropping, is of great concern.

CHAPTER 12 QUESTIONS

1 List some services or facilities, introduced over the past decade, which are dependent on computer systems.

2 Discuss the advantages and disadvantages of the government introducing laws to limit the degree to which computer systems can be used in manufacturing industry.

3 State two advantages for the use of industrial robots and one disadvantage of their use.

4 The introduction of a computer system by an organization sometimes

causes dissatisfaction amongst the staff. Some causes of this dissatisfaction are:

(i) boredom
(ii) frustration
(iii) loss of status
(iv) loss of job or career prospects
(v) changes in patterns of work

(*a*)   Give examples which illustrate each of these causes of dissatisfaction from the computer applications which you have studied.
(*b*)   Describe actions by the management which could have les-
sened or removed each of these causes of dissatisfaction.   (L)

5   When microcomputers are used to automate work, some human jobs
____ _isappear, some will change, and some will be new. If office
___ s automated suggest, with a reason for each:

____ one human job which will disappear
____ ~n job which will change
____ ill appear.   (S)

____ leisure patterns which may develop
____ of computers.

____ erms privacy, integrity and security in

____ nting unauthorized access to computer
____ of preventing corruption of the data.
____ s of the Data Protection Act.
____ es' be more difficult to detect than other
____ or insurance company is robbed, why are
____ t computers were significantly involved?
____ as stored the details of local patients in a
____ two items of data which the system would
____ d be needed.
____ tages of using computers for this purpose.
____ ons why people are worried by the use of
____ sonal data.
____ safeguards which would help to overcome the
____ have.   (N)

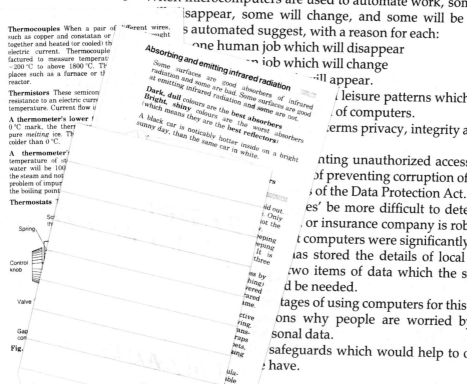

COURSEWORK
COMMENTS

CONTENTS

All the examining groups are required to include an assessment of the candidate's coursework as a factor in determining his final grade. The number of coursework items which each group has stipulated is shown in Appendix 3, which also shows that coursework will account for between 25 per cent and 40 per cent of the total mark. It is therefore an essential contribution to your examination success.

THE RANGE OF PROJECTS

Traditionally, coursework was interpreted as a computer program written by the candidate, but the range of projects which may be submitted within the GCSE regulations is much broader. The emphasis is placed on the ability of the candidate **to use computers sensibly in the solution of appropriate problems and to provide sound explanatory documentation**. Coursework projects will fall into three groups:

1 writing an original program or a number of programs; these may be separate or designed to form an integrated suite of programs.

2 the modification of an existing program or software applications package.

3 the utilization of existing software – this will normally be an applications package.

Before beginning your coursework:

(*a*) **Ensure that you have read the guidelines of the relevant examining group.** Some groups provide very clear principles of coursework presentation and statements of its marking criteria, which are of particular value. If a **standard format** is defined for the presentation of coursework, make sure that you use it. Note any special conditions, such as the maximum project length, which may be applicable.

(*b*) At the time of writing, two Boards are able to supply sample projects which have been marked according to their specified scheme. If such projects are available from your examining group, study them; they will provide a clear indication of the standard which is expected.

(*c*) Look at the objectives in section B of the core syllabus (Appendix 1) which will form the basis of the coursework assessment. Use them. As your coursework proceeds, tick off each as it is adequately covered. They may also be a help to you in planning your coursework, particularly if you intend to submit more than one piece.

(*d*)   Finally, remember throughout your coursework that it will be your explanations and justifications which will be important – it is these aspects of the coursework which demonstrate a clear understanding and command of the work.

PROGRAMMING

The structure of programming coursework is very important. The sequence below is typical of GCSE examining group requirements. At the end of each section is a documentation checklist of points to include in your coursework.

1   **A clear statement of the problem** which you will tackle. Think carefully about the selection of the problem. It should be substantial and possess characteristics which will make it appropriate for solution by the application of computer techniques. Compare your intended solution with the objectives of section B of the core syllabus – how many are covered? Discuss the problem with your teacher; it is expected that candidates will have the guidance of their teachers at this stage. He or she will advise you on the appropriateness of your selection. If the 'output' from your intended project will not be visual, say a control operation or a warning sound, some thought will also need to be given as to how the success of the program will be communicated to the examiner.

DOCUMENTATION CHECKLIST

(1) A clear statement of the problem.
(2) The expected results.

2   **Analysis and solution of the problem.** You should consider the solution of the problem in general terms. There will be no use for programming statements at this stage. If you consider a number of possible methods of solution, point this out to the examiner and justify your eventual choice. Your method of solution will normally be presented as an algorithm, which often takes the form of an outline flowchart; this need not be the case, but the algorithm must be **clearly systematical** and appropriate to the problem.

Example problem: In the game of craps two dice are thrown. A win is obtained by a total of 7 or 11. Design a computer simulation of this game which will roll the dice 100 times. The total number of wins will be displayed on completion of the simulation.

Alternative algorithm structures for this problem are shown below:

A. FLOWCHART

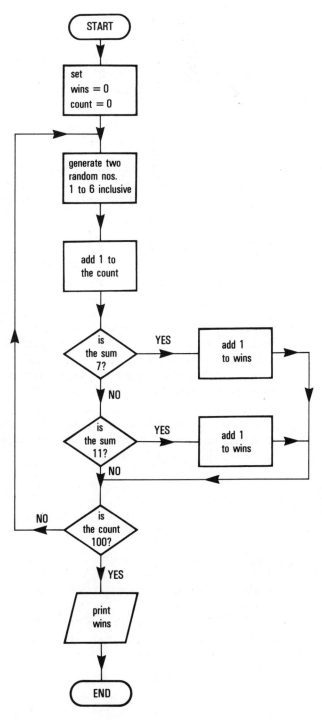

Figure 13.1 Flowchart

B. STATEMENT ALGORITHM

1. Initialize the WINS count.
2. Initialize the total throws COUNT.
3. Generate two random numbers 1 to 6 inclusive.
4. Add 1 to the COUNT.
5. If the random numbers add to 7, add 1 to the WINS.
6. If the random numbers add to 11, add 1 to the WINS.
7. If the COUNT is 100, jump to step 9.
8. Return to step 3.
9. Display the WINS value.
10. End.

In addition, draw attention to any assumptions which your method of solution may make and any **limitations** which you recognize – generated either by the statement of the problem or its solution.

DOCUMENTATION CHECKLIST

(3) The possible methods of solution (justify your choice).
(4) A solution algorithm.
(5) The limitations of the problem or its solutions.
(6) Any assumptions made by your method of solution.

3 **System specification.** Define the hardware components required by your solution. Draw attention to any limitations in your method of solution imposed by hardware restrictions. How will the data be captured? Describe the data preparation. Data should be **encoded**, if appropriate, to make it concise, standardized and unambiguous. The structure of any data files should be defined and justified. **Validation checks** should be included in the solution to check for 'rogue' data or transcription errors. Consider also the output format – will your program offer alternative outputs?

DOCUMENTATION CHECKLIST

(7) Describe the hardware required

(8) Describe the method of data capture and any data pre-paration.

(9) Verification method.

(10) The structure of the data files.

(11) Validation techniques.

(12) Output format.

4 **The actual program implementation** should draw attention to the programming methods which have been used. Many programs, for instance, will include a sort routine, but the examiner will expect some awareness that there are numerous methods of sorting on a computer. The method which you use may need some supporting comments, particularly if it includes additional features such as flags or pointers for greater speed.

Example: The diagrams below illustrate the principles of sorting using the **exchange** and **insertion** sorts. In both cases the numbers are

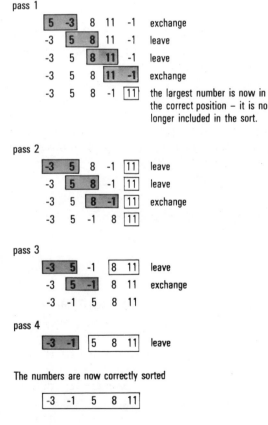

pass 1

5	-3	8	11	-1	exchange
-3	5	8	11	-1	leave
-3	5	8	11	-1	leave
-3	5	8	11	-1	exchange
-3	5	8	-1	11	the largest number is now in the correct position – it is no longer included in the sort.

pass 2

-3	5	8	-1	11	leave
-3	5	8	-1	11	leave
-3	5	8	-1	11	exchange
-3	5	-1	8	11	

pass 3

-3	5	-1	8	11	leave
-3	5	-1	8	11	exchange
-3	-1	5	8	11	

pass 4

| -3 | -1 | 5 | 8 | 11 | leave |

The numbers are now correctly sorted

| -3 | -1 | 5 | 8 | 11 |

Figure 13.3 Exchange sort

sorted into **ascending** order but the algorithm (and programming) is easily changed to reverse the sequence.

The exchange sort is easy to understand and to program, but only appropriate for a relatively small number of data items. The number of comparisons which it makes is directly proportional to the number of items, though the inclusion of a flag which checks that exchanges are taking place may allow premature termination of the full process.

The insertion sort is more difficult to program but more efficient (faster for the same number of data items). The complete set of ordered data is built up by inserting each successive figure into the subset of the data which is already sorted.

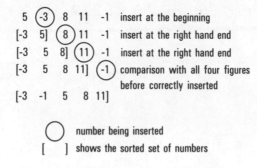

```
 5  (-3)  8   11  -1    insert at the beginning
[-3  5]  (8) 11  -1    insert at the right hand end
[-3  5  8] (11) -1    insert at the right hand end
[-3  5  8  11] (-1)   comparison with all four figures
                       before correctly inserted
[-3  -1  5  8  11]
```

```
 O      number being inserted
[    ]  shows the sorted set of numbers
```

Figure 13.4 Insertion sort

In large data processing applications the data is frequently held in a number of different files which are each sorted independently. The files are then **merged** to complete the sort.

The most common user/operator interface is the keyboard, but you should consider other possible alternatives which may be appropriate to the problem.

DOCUMENTATION CHECKLIST

(13) A description of the programming methods.

(14) An annotated listing of the program.

Testing

The purpose of this section is to demonstrate to the examiner that the program actually works. Choose test data carefully; it should include all the possible input permutations from the problem and also some illegal data. The outcome from the test data **must be known** and compared with that produced from the program. If faults are discovered in the program, use the test data to **dry run** the program in order to locate the error. If unexpected limitations of the program are revealed and corrected, further annotated listings must be made; a complete annotated listing of the final program is essential.

DOCUMENTATION CHECKLIST

(15) Test data.
(16) Sample outputs using the test data.
(17) Additional annotated listings – if required.
(18) Final sample outputs – if required.
(19) The operating instructions (user guide).

Conclusion

The conclusion should present a balanced, global view of the project. The success of the program in solving the problem should be discussed, any further limitations stated and any possible extensions relevant to the original problem considered. Finally, remember that your program must be capable of being understood and used by an examiner totally unfamiliar with the problem or (you should assume) with programming skills. Ensure that the user (and maintenance) instructions are complete and easily understood.

DOCUMENTATION CHECKLIST

(20) Balanced summary of the project.

THE MODIFICATION OF AN EXISTING PROGRAM OR APPLICATIONS PACKAGE

The modification or extension of an existing program is basically programming coursework, except that it will not consist solely of original work.

The reason for its modification will normally arise from its failure to meet particular conditions, i.e. a problem will have been identified for which the existing software is broadly, but not wholly, applicable.

Candidates making this choice should use the detailed guidelines of the previous section but note that:

1 All uses of existing software should be acknowledged.
2 The annotated listings should include the complete program and the existing software should also be annotated to demonstrate to the examiner that it is clearly understood.

THE USE OF EXISTING SOFTWARE

The majority of computer users will use an applications package and the inclusion of this coursework option is a recognition of that fact. The general approach of candidates selecting this option will be very similar to the detailed programming coursework description. The selection of the applications package should be made with care – it must offer sufficient scope for a clear demonstration of your ability.

1 **The problem**. If you choose to use an applications package, select an **appropriate problem** and explain why it is particularly relevant to the

package. Submission of a general description of a package will gain little credit – remember that the emphasis is on the ability of the candidate to use computers sensibly to **solve problems**.

DOCUMENTATION CHECKLIST

(1) A clear statement of the problem.
(2) Why it is appropriate to the package being used.

2 **Analysis and solution of the problem.** The detail of this section will depend on the actual software, but you should clearly indicate the stages involved in progressing towards a solution and what form the output or solution will take. At all stages, any options which are made from those which the software presents should be justified. If a wordprocessing package is used, for instance, the documents which the solution of the problem will require should be defined, their purpose stated and the structure of their storage clarified; will they, for example, be stored as complete documents or composed of existing segments within the system?

DOCUMENTATION CHECKLIST

(3) How the software will be used to solve the problem.
(4) Justify the selection of any options offered by the software.
(5) Define the format of the solution.

3 **System specification.** Discuss the hardware requirements of your solution; if specific hardware is not readily available, e.g. a graph plotter, the selection of an applications package which really demands its availability may be ill-advised. Consider the methods of **data capture** and the structure of their presentation to the software – are there, for instance, any limitations on the field lengths or number of records?

DOCUMENTATION CHECKLIST

(6) The hardware components which your solution requires.
(7) A description of the user interface.
(8) The methods of data capture.
(9) Methods of error reduction, validation checks which the software contains.
(10) The structure of the data presented to the software.

4 **The operation of the software.** This is the heart of the project which uses existing software in relation to the problem. In the use of an information storage and retrieval package, for instance, create records, search records (on more than one field), amend, delete and insert records and sort records by any defined field.

DOCUMENTATION CHECKLIST

(11) Create records, documents.

(12) Provide output showing your ability to:

(i) search, amend, sort records.

(ii) insert, delete or re-position characters, words or paragraphs.

(iii) use the full range of editing facilities.

(13) The range and ease of use of the editing facilities.

(14) The advantages and limitations of the interrogation or command formats.

(15) Comment on any sections of the user documentation which are difficult to understand – explain how these sections could be amended.

4 **Testing.** Demonstrate a complete understanding of the advantages and limitations of the software. If data is required, state and justify a range of test data which will test the system thoroughly in relation to the problem. Where parameters are required – for instance, in a word processing package – demonstrate their effect on the output and any limitation, such as their ability to cope with illegal values.

DOCUMENTATION CHECKLIST

(16) Test data.

(17) Outputs from the test data.

(18) Alternative outputs from the variation of parameters.

Conclusion

A global view of the success of the applications package in relation to the problem. Comment on any additional features which would enhance the software, making it even more appropriate to the problem's solution.

DOCUMENTATION CHECKLIST

(19) A balanced summary.

(20) Specific recommendations to enhance the software package.

GENERAL EXAMINATION HINTS

1 Obtain the relevant examination syllabus. Its main body will be identical to the core syllabus and appropriate additional information detailed in the text analysis, but the syllabus will also define the case study to be examined. You should tick off each of the syllabus statements as it is covered in your revision.

2 Prepare thoroughly for the examination – use the chapter summaries as a final checklist of points.

3   Do all the end-of-chapter questions in this text – they are there as a **supplement** and **reinforcement** of the chapter content.

4   If your examining group provides a brief case study at the time of Paper 1 for examination in Paper 2:

  (i) read it carefully;

  (ii) underline key points;

  (iii) try to anticipate the questions which could be generated by the description or related to it. A general description, for instance, suggests that some questions could include the flow of data through the system, systems flow charts, data preparation, verification and validation procedures and process descriptions, e.g. merging two files. A more detailed description involving the file structure could facilitate questions on encoding, decoding, field lengths, storage media and library routines such as sort routines.

5   Keep yourself up to date. Computing is a rapidly developing field. Well-informed and knowledgeable articles are often found in newspapers and magazines.

6   Read the questions very carefully – more than once. Make sure that you answer the question which is asked and not the question which you would like to answer. Do not 'pick out' key words and write all you know; the examiners will expect organized, relevant and appropriate answers.

7   Use the question mark scheme – it provides a good guide to the depth or length of answer which is required. Generally each relevant point in your answer will be awarded one mark; if eight marks are available for a section, you should make eight clear and distinct points.

CHAPTER 13 QUESTIONS

1   The correct order for the steps involved in the development of a new system is

  (a)   design – documentation – analysis – implementation

  (b)   analysis – documentation – design – implementation

  (c)   implementation – design – analysis – documentation

  (d)   analysis – design – implementation – documentation?

2   Many estate agents now use a computer-based information retrieval system to help answer questions about houses for sale. When new information is added, a data capture form is used and the information is verified and validated.

  (a)   What is a data capture form?

  (b)   Describe one way of verifying the information.

  (c)   Describe one way of validating the information.

  (d)   The estate agent may buy an existing package or commission a software to be written specially. Give two advantages for each method.   (S)

3   Define a program loop. State two methods of terminating a program loop.

4   What do you understand by the terms
    (*a*)   test data?
    (*b*)   subroutine?
5   What is meant by a data terminator?
6   The flow-chart on page 203 shows the steps in the execution of a
    program stored in the memory of a simple single address machine. In
    this machine each instruction occupies one memory location.
    (*a*)   Draw a ring around the box in the flow-chart which will be
    obeyed immediately an unconditional jump is executed.

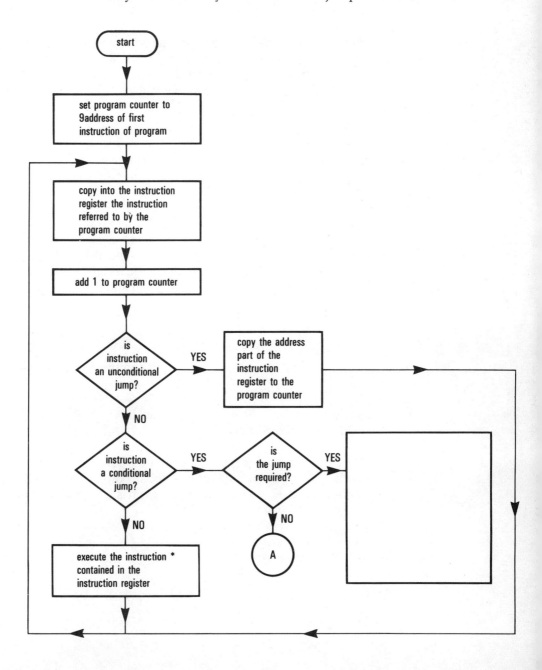

(b)   After each instruction has been fetched, 1 is added to the program counter. Why is this necessary for most instructions?

(c)   Complete the blank box in the flow chart to show what happens in the case of a conditional jump.

(d)   On the flow chart, mark the point to which the connector symbol A should lead. Explain your answer.

(e)   Give an example of an instruction which would cause the box labelled * to be obeyed.

7   (a)   Describe the operation of the exchange sort. Illustrate your ansawer by sorting the set of numbers 4, 8, −9. 7, −3, −5 using this method.

(b)   Why is the sort unsuitable for a large number of data items?

8   MAX is a local variable in the procedure SORT.

(a)   What is meant by the expression 'local variable'?

(b)   Explain the need for local variables.   (M)

ANSWERS TO
TEXT QUESTIONS

CHAPTER 1

1 See text.
2 Microcomputer – a small business for its stock control or correspondence (wordprocessing system).
   Minicomputer – a local authority or chain of stores using a central
computer for stock control.
   Mainframe – large insurance and banking institutions.
3 See text.
4 Analogue.
5 Input device, processing unit, output device, backing storage.
6 See text.
7 See text.
8 See text.
9 Because of the limitation in size of the main store.
10 Process control – see real-time processing in the applications section.

CHAPTER 2

1 See text.
2 A light pen.
3 A parity bit ensures that all the character representations have either
an odd or even number of 1s. It is used to eliminate hardware
malfunction or communications errors, by counting the number of 1s
in each character representation and ensuring that the total is con-
sistent with the parity.
4 Keyboard.
5 See text.
6 It is easier to work freehand with a mouse.
7 Design applications – possibly the graphics department in a school.
8 Daisywheel – wordprocessing system.
   Dot matrix – education or small business applications.
   Laser – large-scale printing operations, e.g. 'junk' mail applications.
9 Quiet and fast. No hard copy and prolonged use could lead to health
risks.
10 See text.

11 (a) Laser scanner
   (b) Mouse
   (c) OCR
   (d) OMR
   (e) Modem
   (f) Microfiche
12 (a) Cheques
   (b) By a magnetic ink character reader
   (c) Magnetic ink character recognition (MICR)

CHAPTER 3

1 Magnetic tape – security copies.
   Magnetic disc – large enquiry services, e.g. British Rail.
2 ROM contains the language interpreter and utility software. Additional ROMs may also be installed, e.g. a wordprocessing chip.
3 See text.
4 See text.
5 The main part of the program is in store. When each special operation is needed the required software is loaded from disc to main memory, overwriting any software which is already in memory for another operation.
6 For example, faster loading and storage of software. Programs or data exceeding the main memory capacity can be used realistically.
7 They are non-volatile.
8 Staff can train independently at their own pace. The high cost of mastering a videodisc is a disadvantage.
9 Payroll – each record is used in turn and the processing can be done when other demands on the computer system are low, e.g. at night.
   Bank account records connected to cashpoint terminals – rapid access is required on an unpredictable basis.

CHAPTER 4

1 122
2 100011_2
3 See text.
4 31, 011111_2
5 011011, 100101
6 011011, 111011
7 $1110_\uparrow$, $1111_\uparrow1$, $111_\uparrow111$

$0_\uparrow011100101$, $0_\uparrow111110100$, $0_\uparrow111110011$

Retaining 4 bits for the mantissa it is impossible to have an exact representation of 7.875 (this would be 01111110011, i.e. 11 bits); the least significant bit is therefore omitted to gain the most acceptable error (0.125).

8 See text.
9 See text; -128 to 127; 128 (leaving one bit for parity).
10

P	Q	R
0	1	1
0	0	0
0	1	1
0	0	0
0	1	1
0	0	0
1	1	1
1	0	1

11 P=1 for the rows 0101, 0110, 0111.

CHAPTER 5

1 Reading bar codes.
2 See text.
3 See text.
4 Assume that the code number of stock items is being input along with their cost. Validation checks (*a*) check digit; (*b*) hash total on code; (*c*) range check on the code. A correct code with incorrect cost could be input.
5 See text.
6 See text.
7 (*a*)   See text.
   (*b*)   See text.
   (*c*)   Employee leaves; new employee; employee's status changes, e.g. she is married.
   (*d*)   Search.
8 See text.
9 See text.
10 See text.
11 SORT arranges the new items of stock in the same order as the master file.
        MERGE joins together the old master file and the file of new stock to form a new master file of stock.

CHAPTER 6

1 See text.
2 See text.
3 1; 2.
4 See text.
5 See text.
6   (i) The variation in dialects.
         (ii) The operating system.
7 See text.

8   (i) Payroll.

(ii) Product distribution systems.

(iii) Stock control.

N.B. A very large variety of applications programs is now available.

9   (*a*)   (i) 10 PRUNT A

20 LET C=(5

(ii) 10 PRINT A

20 LET C=(5)

(*b*)   Compiler; interpreter.

(*c*)   Retype the line.

(*d*)   Invalid input; subscript too big.

(*e*)   Jump to wrong place although the instruction is legal. Dry running.

10   Compilers and interpreters enable a computer to execute programs written in high-level languages (1) by translating them to machine language (1). This enables the use of languages appropriate to the problem (1) without needing to know about the internal workings of the machine.

A syntax error breaks a rule of language and hence does not produce understandable machine instructions (1).

An execution error comes from trying to carry out an impossible task (1) +example (1).

An interpreter obeys instructions as they come to him (1), although obvious errors will be detected (2). A compiler has to translate the whole program (1) to object code and will detect errors before starting execution (1).

An interpreter has helpful error messages (1); good restarting more tolerant of errors (1); compiler detects all syntax errors (1).

Compiled code executes quickly (1); guaranteed syntax error free (1); code to be interpreted, which will then occupy less space (1).

CHAPTER 7

1   See text.

2   iii, i, ii, iii.

3   See text.

4   (*a*)   Multiple, simultaneous users.

(*b*)   File protection; undesirable use.

(*c*)   File owner; permitted user; private information barred to an unauthorized user.

(*d*)   Give time to each; protect against mutual corruption; logging.

5   See text.

6   See text.

7   See text.

8   (*a*)   Real-time processing involves receiving continuously changing data and processing it sufficiently rapidly to be able to influence the source of data (2).

(*b*)   For example, chemical manufacturing process.

(c)   Source, type and purpose of the data (3); realistic method (2); use of interface (1); validation (1); logical transformation of input to output (4); logically necessary outputs (2); conversion method (2). (See description of a chemical process in chapter 11.)

CHAPTER 8

1   See text.
2   See text.
3   (a)   Prestel.
    (b)   Modem or acoustic coupler.
            To change signals from the computer into a form suitable for transmission over the telephone network.
    (c)   Teleshopping; home banking.
    (d)   Interactive; far greater store of information.
4   See text.
5   See text.
6   Speed; the system will inform you if a message is waiting.
        No certainty that the person to whom the message is sent will access his mail regularly – also the small number of users at present.
7   (a)   Will arrive more quickly.
    (b)   Message can be left waiting if receiver is not there.
    (c)   Fewer letters posted, therefore fewer postal workers will be needed.
    (d)   Parcel.
8   See text.
9   Virtually any business, central or local administration housed mainly in a single building
            (i) The computer users (or potential users) are in relatively close geographical proximity.
            (ii) The users have occasional requirement for powerful, expensive peripherals, e.g. line printers.
10 See text.
11 See text.

CHAPTER 9

1   See text.
2   Becoming a programmer is the first promotion. With further qualifications the post of systems analyst or chief programmer may be possible.
3   Key-to-disc has replaced the transciption of data on to punched cards.
4   See text.
5   Liaison with systems analysts; overall control of the section; monitoring the quality of work and the allocation of specific programming tasks.
6   Probably educated to graduate level, with additional data processing

experience including systems design. He will enjoy working with people and have the ability quickly to build up their confidence and co-operation – this is vital, because a major aspect of his role involves working with people to analyse their tasks; and possibly to require them, ultimately, to learn new skills.

7 No computer staff required.
   Expensive resources are shared.
   Complete control over procedures.
   Tailored processing software.
8 See text.
9 Train staff; prepare computer room; re-organize methods of working.
10 See text.
11 See text.

CHAPTER 10

CASE STUDY 1

1 See text.
2 See text.
3 It is the key field for each record.
4 See p.77. The check digit is the most commonly applied validation check to reference numbers.
5 It would have performed the data preparation automatically by, for instance, recording the times on a punched card.
6 A computer bureau offers computing services.
   Customer advantages: no computer staff required, the (shared) use of expensive hardware.
   Customer disadvantages: limited control of the processing, security, turnaround time and lack of control over the costs.
7 Calculated during processing: only the rate £609. The rate in the pound is not a standing detail, but it is set by the Council not calculated.
8 See p.156.
9 For security.
10 Letters which are frequently used and have a very similar structure, so that they can be constructed from a number of stored paragraphs.
11 To show the overall financial analysis and to predict the effect of rate changes.

CASE STUDY 2

1 See text.
2 See text.
3 Reference number.
4 351012.
5 Size 16; hire charge £45; the sixth size 16 dress purchased.
6 To facilitate faster searching.
7 Display a single record.

8 See text.
9 To enable her to make copies easily – for security.
10 Both the old and the new system are in operation simultaneously.
11 Either a daisywheel (excellent print quality) or a dot matrix (cheaper and more versatile).
12 F4=B4*C4; G4=B4*D4+E4.

CHAPTER 11

1 See text.
2 Input – code identifying each cow.
   Process – measure the yield.
   Storage – floppy disc.
   Output – updating of the records, a visual display of the yield and possibly a printout (dot matrix printer).
3 Both are on-line, but in real-time processing the sole purpose is the single process (no time sharing); any delay is vital. Interactive processing is rapid, but a short delay is not crucial – time-sharing is a feature.
4 See text.
5 See text.
6 See p.156.
7 The computer executes an instruction and then tests an interrupt register. It continues to do this until the clock sends the interrupt register a signal which sets one of the bits to 1. When it next tests this register, the computer finds the 1, so it reads the temperature and resets the interrupt register and then continues processing as before.
8 Advantage: discs can be used on another micro; can use micro anywhere; private data is secure.
   Disadvantage: cannot easily combine with other firms; limited range of software.
9 (a) bar codes; needs little training, reliable.
   (b) Unique to the book, fixed length validation, ease of input, i.e. only 10 characters needed.
   (c) selling lists to commercial concerns.

CHAPTER 12

1 See text.
2 See text.
3 Robots will work in environments potentially damaging to human health for prolonged periods.
   Initial cost.
4   (i) Boredom – probably job being reduced to repetitive work.
         (ii) Frustration – lack of control of the system.
         (iii) Loss of status – division of labour meaning that people no longer take part in the whole process.

(iv) Department downgraded; best people work directly with the computer.

(v) Work patterns – have to fit in with the computer, loss of flexibility, change of environment, e.g. use of VDUs.

(*a*)   Examples must illustrate the point; many can be taken for the same application. The application could well be one not very suitable for computer application or not well implemented.

(*b*)   Responses will depend on the cause. Marks to be given for sensible suggestions, probably involving better consultation and planning.

5   (*a*)   Filing clerk – replaced by information retrieval.

(*b*)   Typist – change to word processing.

(*f45c*)   *Computer operator – to run programs.*

6   See text.

7   See text.

8   See text.

9   See text.

10   The crime may involve extremely small individual amounts taken from a large number of accounts over a lengthy period of time, or one code among the many thousands which are processed. Because of the fear of public loss of confidence.

11   (*a*)   Medical history; reference to any drug allergies – to assist the doctor in making his prescriptions.

(*b*)   Rapid access (from remote points if necessary) and the records can be called by the doctor for display on his desk terminal; there is no need for the physical movement of files.

(*c*)   Unauthorized access; incorrect contents.

(*d*)   See text.

CHAPTER 13

1   d.

2   (*a*)   A form completed by the customer or staff, then copied from when data is input.

(*b*)   Record displayed after input and may be confirmed or corrected.

(*c*)   Each item of information entered is tested to ensure it is correct type, size and, for numeric fields, lies between pre-defined limits.

(*d*)   Immediately available; error-free; tailored to requirements; may be sold to other users.

3   A sequence of programs which are executed repeatedly.

Terminated by a specified condition – either a set count value is reached or a rogue data item is encountered.

4   Test data is data used to test a program or flow chart. Its outcome is known and its range will test the program for all feasible input permutations.

5   Value at the end of a set of data used to stop an input loop.

6   (*a*)   Copy address box.

     (*b*)   So that the next instruction is fetched from the next location.

     (*c*)   Change program counter to address of next instruction. Nothing has to be done, so just fetch next instruction.

     (*e*)   Any non-jump instruction, e.g. LET P=P+1.

7   See text.

8   (*a*)   The variable is only used in the procedure where it is local and it cannot be used outside.

     (*b*)   It enables a library of procedures to be developed by different programmers, who can use the same variable names without confusion.

THE CORE CONTENT

The core content must be included in every syllabus. The table showing the text analysis (p.11) reveals that there are few differences in syllabus content between the Examining Groups. There are, however, marked differences in the detailed method of examination and the proportion of the marks which are allocated to each objective by the different Groups. These differences are shown in Appendix 2.

There are five assessment objectives.

ASSESSMENT OBJECTIVE A

The candidate should be able to demonstrate a knowledge and understanding of the techniques needed to solve problems related to practical applications.

Candidates should be able to:

A1 Derive the information requirements of a system and specify a system precisely in terms of the output needed, the input data and any necessary files.

A2 Formulate and communicate in appropriate ways, methods of solution of problems.

A3 Describe and justify suitable methods of communication between people and systems.

A4 Explain the need for encoding information for computer processing.

A5 Demonstrate a knowledge of documentation and an understanding of the use of documentation.

A6 Explain the need for adequate testing of solutions.

A7 Interpret information about systems presented in a variety of ways.

ASSESSMENT OBJECTIVE B

The candidate should be able to use computers sensibly to produce solutions to appropriate problems, and to document their solutions.

This includes the design of a simple system. Candidates should be able to:

B1 Derive the information requirements for the solution of a problem in terms of the output needed, the input data and any necessary files.

B2 Encode data and information for processing on a computer.

B3 Select suitable methods of communication between people and the computer.

B4 Formulate and test algorithms.

B5 Use a computer to implement the algorithm satisfactorily.

B6 Document his/her work using appropriate methods of communication.

ASSESSMENT OBJECTIVE C

The candidate should be able to demonstrate a knowledge and understanding of the functions of the main hardware and software components of a computer system and their relationships with the representation of stored data and programs.
Candidates should be able to:

C1 Explain the functions of the component parts of a computer configuration.

C2 Evaluate the suitability of current input, output and storage devices in particular applications.

C3 Explain the use of interface devices which enable computers to communicate with other devices, including computers.

C4 Describe the characteristics of the various levels of programming languages.

C5 Explain the need for translation programs.

C6 Describe the functions of operating systems.

C7 Compare the purposes of utility programs and applications packages and identify their appropriate uses.

C8 Reporesent integer, characters and instructions in computer format.

The candidate should be able to demonstrate a knowledge and understanding of the range and scope of computer applications. Candidates should be able to:

D1 Identify the steps involved in the analysis, design, implementation and documentation of a system.

D2 Describe the various methods of collection, verification and validation of data and the presentation of results, and justify the choice of appropriate methods for given applications.

D3 Describe the organization and manipulation of data files.

D4 Explain the need for various modes of computer operation which are suitable for particular types of processing.

D5 Identify the tasks of various personnel involved in the operation of a system.

D6 Select and describe specific applications illustrating the objectives above.

The candidate should be able to demonstrate some understanding of the social and economic effects of the use of computerized systems on individuals, organizations and society and formulate a reasoned view of the potential benefits and drawbacks of computer usage.

WEIGHTING OF THE OBJECTIVES IN THE ASSESSMENT

1   The table below shows the minimum and maximum percentages which must be applied to each of the assessment objectives in Appendix 1.

2   Timed, written papers will constitute at least 60 per cent of the total assessment.

Assessment Objective	A	B	C	D	E
Minimum and Maximum %	15–20	25–30	15–20	20–30	10–15

THE EXAMINING GROUP SCHEMES OF ASSESSMENT

LONDON AND EAST ANGLIAN GROUP

Written examination

Differentiated papers – either one or two papers each 1½ hours.
   The Case Study is an additional paper – 2 hours. (Detail of the Case Study is provided at the time of the first paper and examined in the second.) 35% of total marks.

Coursework – one concise project 5 to 15 sides of A4 in total length. 30% of the total marks.

THE MIDLAND EXAMINING GROUP

Written examination

Differentiated papers – one or two papers are required, each 1 hour.
   The Case Study is an additional 1-hour paper counting 25% of the total marks.

Coursework – one or more pieces of work. 25% of total marks.

THE NORTHERN EXAMINING ASSOCIATION

Written examination

Two common papers, each of which consists of compulsory questions.

Paper 1: 1¼ hours	30% of total marks
Paper 2: 2 hours	30% of total marks

These papers include questions on the designated case study.

Coursework – one piece – 40% of total marks.

THE SOUTHERN EXAMINING GROUP

Written examination

Three common papers:

Paper 1 (objective test)	45 minutes	20% of total marks.
Paper 2 (general)	1½ hours	30% of total marks.
Paper 3 (case study)	1 hour	20% of total marks.

Coursework – one project to a maximum length of 10 sides of A4. 30% of total marks.

THE WELSH JOINT EDUCATION COMMITTEE

Written examination

Differentiated papers – two papers are required, one of 1½ hours and one of 2 hours. Their combination is 70% of the total marks.

No specific Case Study is defined.

Coursework – two projects, each counting 15% of the total marks.